THE BOOK OF FIVE RINGS

Complete Version + A Growth Path for the Man of Today.

CONTENTS:

THE BOOK OF FIVE RINGS

INTRODUCTION

Rude, bold, cunning, fearless, Miyamoto Musashi embodied the figure of the greatest swordsman of all times even in his lifetime and soon became a true legend for the Japanese. When he was only 13 years old he fought his first duel and killed his opponent. From then on his life was totally intertwined with the art of the sword, even though he did not reject the use of other weapons, such as when, cleverly adapting to the situation, he used the oar of a boat to defeat a famous samurai armed with a long sword. After the historic battle of Sekigahara in 1600, in which he took part on the side of the defeated, he became a ronin, a wandering samurai with long hair, without a master to whom he swore loyalty and allegiance, but acknowledging honour and glory only to himself in over sixty duels that he always won. When in his old age he retired to a cave, his end point became writing, and as he put aside his sword, he took up the brush with the same mastery. Guided by enlightenment, meditating on the profound meaning of life with mental clarity and attention, he created this extraordinary practical and spiritual testament, which he finished in 1645, dying shortly afterwards at the age of 62. On a hasty reading it seems a meticulous and almost pedantic best practice essay on the art of the sword, but in reality it is a path of knowledge where the five rings represent the cycle of the five elements that make up the world. Earth defines the fundamentals of strategy,

1

Water presents new battle tactics, Fire a study of conflict, Wind compares other schools of war and the importance of knowing your opponent, and Emptiness the combination of teachings and the spiritual formation of a warrior. This path according to Musashi is the way of Heiho, the inevitable way of the samurai, which is to win at all costs when one's own life is at risk. For us, living in the West , it is almost natural to associate Musashi and his Japan with the world in France at that time, made famous by equally impenitent and guascon characters such as Charles de Batz de Castelmore d'Artagnan, the protagonist of the novel "The three Musketeers" set in 1600 by Alexandre Dumas, or the great and suffering theatrical figure of Cyrano de Bergerac, a fine poet and unbeatable swordsman. However, although they shared the same virtues of honour and loyalty to the sovereign, the basic differences were obvious. In the world of the 'singolar tenzone' to which d'Artagnan and even more Cyrano belonged , the female figure was exalted and made the protagonist, a conception completely foreign to the samurai world, but moreover, and above all, it lacked the inner depth expressed in perfection, in the beauty of the gesture and in the supreme attention that were the basis of Musashi's teaching. It is even more distant from the "Hagakure", considered the gospel of the samurai, written at the beginning of 1700s by Yamamoto Tsunetomo, himself a samurai and then a Zen monk, developed as a collection of aphorisms and moral and practical principles where the underlying theme is the death of the ego rather than the physical death. A pivotal text in Japanese culture, whose traits it has partly forged, also treasured by kamikazes who kept it with them until the last moment of their lives. The way of the samurai (mushin) followed by both Musashi and Tsunetomo, steeped in the Zen Buddhist tradition, stood outside dualism, the discrimination of this rather than that, a fundamental approach in the art of the sword as in all martial arts. The Hagakure in particular celebrates the praise of folly of the samurai who is already dead before dying because his ego is no longer there: 'A samurai must be proud to have such courage in going towards his death like a madman'. Both masters believed that "thought hinders the perfect action which is carried out spontaneously", therefore "it is good to proceed without wavering, without stopping to think for a long time, with courage without ever getting tired because in battle a mind full of doubts will do no good". The concept of calculating thought was taken up in a modern key by Martin Heidegger, a twentieth-century philosopher, where calculating means utilitarian, whereby weighing up gain and loss, hesitating in time, one prefers life rather than death, and thus can never produce the courage that can only be realised in the instant itself.

Musashi's Japan saw the affirmation of the Tokugawa daimyo shogunate, winners at Sekigahara, who put an end to centuries of civil wars, and the following was an era of centralised feudalism that ended in 1868-69 following the 'forced' opening to the West. During this long period of time Japan enjoyed stability and relative social peace, despite uprising attempts by some local daimyo, who, being aristocrats, could not stand this centralisation of power. At the same time, in order to combat and repress the phenomenon of banditry, which gradually spread from the countryside to the cities, it was necessary to almost militarise them, in particular Edo, today's Tokyo. At that time, the samurai represented a quantitatively large force, and while progressively losing their authority they were often forced to reinvent themselves in the state bureaucracy or in police activities. It is not by chance that the two main texts on the samurai spirit or Bushido (The Book of the Five Rings and the Hagakure) were written in this period, theorising its purity, with the aim of restoring dignity and vigour to a caste that made the art of war its reason for living. Europe was in a similar situation in some respects, scourged by the Thirty Years' War (1618-1648) which began because of religious issues between the Catholic emperor of the Holy Roman Empire and a large group of German Protestant princes, then turned into a struggle of pure political supremacy of all against all that devastated the entire continent and particularly Germany, which lost half its population. Italy was not spared and after having been the theatre of conflict between the French and the Spanish, with the victory of the latter it began an inexorable decline after almost five hundred years of growth and having been a reference point for the entire western world. There was a return to feudalism with the introduction of sharecropping in the countryside, general impoverishment, demographic decline, under heavy Spanish oppression; a period of decadence with a plurality of states controlled by the Spanish with the exception of the Kingdom of Savoy and the Republic of Venice. Numerous popular uprisings broke out, including Milan of Manzoni's memory, Palermo, Messina, which was besieged for two years, and above all Naples with the revolt led by Masaniello, a well-known popular hero figure, which were eventually crushed by the Spanish power allied with the local aristocracy. As Benedetto Croce well argued, an empire in asphyxiation repressed an equally ruined country in a century, the 17th century, which was now the prerogative of the new and dynamic Protestant powers, first and foremost Holland, soon to be joined by England. In Italy, like in Japan, brigandage raged as much as impunity, so that everyone tended to take the law into their own hands, and many Italians of the time had many similarities with the figure of the samurai. They were the proud heirs of a school of fencing and sword forging unique in Europe, highly skilled swordsmen able to manoeuvre in a really hostile environment, where power switched frequently from one to the other and it was vital to know how to defend or attack. Historically, it should be remembered that many Italians went to swell the ranks of the tercios, an elite corps of the Spanish army made up mostly of lower-ranking nobles or cadets who sought glory and honours through war, fighting all over Europe against the Dutch Protestants or the Turks in the Mediterranean.

CHAPTER 1

THE GROUND BOOK

Strategy is the craft of the warrior. Commanders must enact the craft, and troopers should know this Way. There is no warrior in the world today who really understands the Way of Strategy. There are various Ways. There is the Way of salvation by the law of Buddha, the Way of Confucius governing the Way of learning, the Way of healing as a doctor, as a poet teaching the Way of Waka, tea, archery, and many arts and skills. Each man practices as he feels inclined. It is said the warrior's is the twofold Way of pen and sword, and he should have a taste for both Ways. Even if a man has no natural ability he can be a warrior by sticking assiduously to both divisions of the Way. Generally speaking, the Way of the warrior is resolute acceptance of death. Although not only warriors but priests, women, peasants and lowlier folk have been known to die readily in the cause of duty or out of shame, this is a different thing. The warrior is different in that studying the Way of Strategy is based on overcoming men. By victory gained in crossing swords with individuals, or enjoining battle with large numbers, we can attain power and fame for ourselves or our lord. This is the virtue of strategy. The Way of Strategy In China and Japan practitioners of the Way have been known as "masters of strategy". Warriors must learn this Way. Recently there have been people getting on in the world as strategists, but they are usually just swordfencers. The attendants of the Kashima Kantori shrines of the province Hitachi received instruction from the gods, and made schools based on this teaching, traveling from country to country instructing men. This is the recent meaning of strategy. In olden times strategy was listed among the Ten Abilities and Seven Arts as a beneficial practice. It was certainly an art but as a beneficial 4 practice it was not limited to sword-fencing. The true value of swordfencing cannot be seen within the confines of sword-fencing technique. If we look at the world we see arts for sale. Men use equipment to sell their own selves. As if with the nut and the flower, the nut has become less than th flower. In this kind of Way of Strategy, both those teaching and those learning the way are concerned with colouring and showing off their technique, trying to hasten the bloom of the flower. They speak of "This Dojo" and "That Dojo". They are looking for profit. Someone once said "Immature strategy is the cause of grief". That was a true saying. There are four Ways in which men pass through life: as gentlemen, farmers, artisans and merchants. The Way of the farmer. Using agricultural instruments, he sees springs through to autumns with an eye on the changes of season. Second is the Way of the merchant. The wine maker obtains his ingredients and puts them to use to make his living. The Way of the merchant is always to live by taking profit. This is the Way of the merchant. Thirdly the gentleman warrior, carrying the weaponry of his Way. The Way of the warrior is to master the virtue of his weapons. If a

gentleman dislikes strategy he will not appreciate the
benefit of weaponry, so must he not have a little taste
for this? Fourthly the Way of the artisan. The Way of the
carpenter is to become proficient in the use of his tools,
first to lay his plans with a true measure and then
perform his work according to plan. Thus he passes
through life. These are the four Ways of the gentleman,
the farmer, the artisan and the merchant. Comparing
the Way of the Carpenter to Strategy The comparison
with carpentry is through the connection with houses.
Houses of the nobility, houses of warriors, the Four
houses, ruin of houses, thriving of houses, the style of
the house, the tradition of the house, and the name of
the house. The carpenter uses a master plan of the
building, and the Way of Strategy is similar in that there
is a plan of campaign. If you want to learn the craft of
war, ponder over this book. The teacher is as a needle,
the disciple is as thread. You must practice constantly.
Like the foreman carpenter, the commander must know
natural rules, and the rules of the country, and the rules
of houses. This is the Way of the foreman. The foreman
carpenter must know the architectural theory of towers
and temples, and the plans of palaces, and must employ
men to raise up 5 houses. The Way of the foreman
carpenter is the same as the Way of the commander of
a warrior house. In the construction of houses, choice
of woods is made. Straight un-knotted timber of good
appearance is used for the revealed pillars, straight
timber with small defects is used for the inner pillars.
Timbers of the finest appearance, even if a little weak,

is used for the thresholds, lintels, doors, and sliding doors, and so on. Good strong timber, though it be gnarled and knotted, can always be used discreetly in construction. Timber which is weak or knotted throughout should be used as scaffolding, and later for firewood. The foreman carpenter allots his men work according to their ability. Floor layers, makers of sliding doors, thresholds and lintels, ceilings and so on. Those of poor ability lay the floor joists, and those of lesser ability carve wedges and do such miscellaneous work. If the foreman knows and deploys his men well the finished work will be good. The foreman should take into account the abilities and limitations of his men, circulating among them and asking nothing unreasonable. He should know their morale and spirit, and encourage them when necessary. This is the same as the principle of strategy. The Way of Strategy Like a trooper, the carpenter sharpens his own tools. He carries his equipment in his tool box, and works under the direction of his foreman. He makes columns and girders with an axe, shapes floorboards and shelves with a plane, cuts fine openwork and carvings accurately, giving as excellent a finish as his skill will allow. This is the craft of the carpenters. When the carpenter becomes skilled and understands measures he can become a foreman. The carpenter's attainment is, having tools which will cut well, to make small shrines, writing shelves, tables, paper lanterns, chopping boards and pot-lids. These are the specialties of the carpenter. Things are similar for the trooper. You ought to think deeply about this. The attainment of the carpenter is that his work is not warped, that the joints are not misaligned, and that the work is truly planed so that it meets well and is not merely finished in sections. This is essential. If you want to learn this Way, deeply consider the things written in this book one at a time. You must do sufficient research. Outline of the Five Books of this Book of Strategy 6 The Way is shown as five books concerning different aspects. These are Ground, Water, Fire, Wind (tradition), and Void (the illusionary nature of worldly things) The body of the Way of Strategy from the viewpoint of my Ichi school is explained in the Ground book. It is difficult to realize the true Way just through sword-fencing. Know the smallest things and the biggest things, the shallowest things and the deepest things. As if it were a straight road mapped out on the ground, the first book is called the Ground book. Second is the Water book. With water as the basis, the spirit becomes like water. Water adopts the shape of its receptacle, it is sometimes a trickle and sometimes a wild sea. Water has a clear blue colour. By the clarity, things of Ichi school are shown in this book. If you master the principles of sword-fencing, when you freely beat one man, you beat any man in the world. The spirit of defeating a man is the same for ten million men. The strategist makes small things into big things, like building a great Buddha from a one foot model. I cannot write in detail how this is done. The principle of strategy is having one thing, to know ten thousand things. Things of Ichi school are written in this the Water book. Third is the Fire book. This book is about fighting. The spirit of fire is fierce, whether the fire be small or big; and so it is with battles. The Way of battles is the same for man to man fights and for ten thousand a side battles. You must appreciate that spirit can become big or small. What is big is easy to perceive: what is small is difficult to perceive. In short, it is difficult for large numbers of men to change position, so their movements can be easily predicted. An individual can easily change his mind, so his movements are difficult to predict. You must appreciate this. The essence of this book is that you must train day and night in order to make quick decisions. In strategy it is necessary to treat training as part of normal life with your spirit unchanging. Thus combat in battle is described in the Fire book. Fourthly the Wind book. This book is not concerned with my Ichi school but with other schools of strategy. By Wind I mean old traditions, present-day traditions, and family traditions of strategy. Thus I clearly explain the strategies of the world. This is tradition. It is difficult to know yourself if you do not know others. To all Ways there are side-tracks. If you study a Way daily, and your spirit diverges, you may think you are obeying a good Way but objectively it is not the true Way. If you are following the true way and diverge a little, this will later become a large divergence. You must realize this. Other strategies have come to be thought of as mere sword-fencing, and it is not unreasonable that this 7 should be so. The benefit of my strategy, although it includes sword-fencing, lies in a separate principle. I have explained what is commonly meant by strategy in other schools in the Tradition (Wind) book. Fifthly, the book of the Void. By void I mean that which has no beginning and no end. Attaining this principle means not attaining the principle. The Way of strategy is the Way of nature. When you appreciate the power of nature, knowing rhythm of any situation, you will be able to hit the enemy naturally and strike naturally. All this is the Way of the Void. I intend to show how to follow the true Way according to nature in the book of the Void. The Name Ichi Ryu Ni To (One school - two swords) Warriors, both commanders and troopers, carry two swords at their belt. In olden times these were called the long sword and the sword; nowadays they are known as the sword and the companion sword. Let it suffice to say that in our land, whatever the reason, a warrior carries two swords at his belt. It is the Way of the warrior. "Nito Ichi Ryu" shows the advantages of using both swords. The spear and the halberd are weapons which are carried out of doors. Students of the Ichi school Way of Strategy should train from the start with the sword and the long sword in either hand. This is a truth: when you sacrifice your life, you must make fullest use of your weaponry. It is false not to do so, and to die with a weapon yet undrawn. If you hold a sword with both hands, it is difficult to wield it freely to left and right, so my method is to carry the sword in one hand. This does not apply to large weapons such as the spear or halberd, but swords and companion swords can be carried in one hand. It is encumbering to hold a sword in both hands when you are on horseback, when running on uneven roads, on swampy ground, muddy rice fields, stony ground, or in a crowd of people. To hold the long sword in both hands is not the true Way, for if you carry a bow or spear or other arms in your left hand you have only one hand free for the long sword. However, when it is difficult to cut an enemy down with one hand, you must use both hands. It is not difficult to wield a sword in one hand; the Way to learn this is to train with two long swords, one in each hand. It will seem difficult at first, but everything is difficult at first. Bows are difficult to draw, halberds are difficult to wield; as you become accustomed to the bow so your pull will become stronger. When you become used to wielding the long sword, you will gain the power of the Way and wield the sword well. 8 As I will explain in the second book, the Water Book, there is no fast way of wielding the long sword. The long sword should be wielded broadly and the companion sword closely. This is the first thing to realize. According to this Ichi school, you can win with a long weapon, and yet you can also win with a short weapon. In short, the Way of the Ichi school is the spirit of winning, whatever the weapon and whatever its size. It is better to use two swords rather than one when you are fighting a crowd, and especially if you want to take a prisoner. These things cannot be explained in detail. From one thing, know ten thousand things. When you attain the Way of Strategy there will not be one thing you cannot see. You must study hard. The Benefit of the

Two Characters Reading "Strategy" Masters of the long sword are called strategists. As for the other military arts, those who master the bow are called archers, those who master the spear are called spearmen, those who master the gun are called marksmen, those who master the halberd are called halberdiers. But we do not call masters of the Way of the long sword "longswordsmen", nor do we speak of "companion swordsmen". Because bows, guns, spears and halberds are all warriors' equipment they are certainly part of strategy. To master the virtue of the long sword is to govern the world and oneself, thus the long sword is the basis of strategy. The principle is "strategy by means of the long sword". If he attains the virtue of the long sword, one man can beat ten men. Just as one man can beat ten, so a hundred men can beat a thousand, and a thousand can beat ten thousand. In my strategy, one man is the same as ten thousand, so this strategy is the complete warrior's craft. The Way of the warrior does not include other Ways, such as Confucianism, Buddhism, certain traditions, artistic accomplishments and dancing. But even though these are not part of the Way, if you know the Way broadly you will see it in everything. Men must polish their particular Way. The Benefit of Weapons in Strategy There is a time and place for use of weapons. The best use of the companion sword is in a confined space, or when you are engaged closely with an opponent. The long sword can be used effectively in all situations. 9 The halberd is inferior to the spear on the battlefield. With the spear you can take the initiative; the halberd is defensive. In the hands of one of two men of equal ability, the spear gives a little extra strength. Spear and halberd both have their uses, but neither is very beneficial in confined spaces. They cannot be used for taking a prisoner. They are essentially weapons for the field. Anyway, if you learn "indoor" techniques, you will think narrowly and forget the true Way. Thus you will have difficulty in actual encounters. The bow is tactically strong at the commencement of battle, especially battles on a moor, as it is possible to shoot quickly from among the spearmen. However, it is unsatisfactory in sieges, or when the enemy is more than forty yards away. For this reason there are nowadays few traditional schools of archery. There is little use nowadays for this kind of skill. From inside fortifications, the gun has no equal among weapons. It is the supreme weapon on the field before the ranks clash, but once swords are crossed the gun becomes useless. One of the virtues of the bow is that you can see the arrows in flight and correct your aim accordingly, whereas gunshot cannot be seen. You must appreciate the importance of this. Just as a horse must have endurance and no defects, so it is with weapons. Horses should walk strongly, and swords and companion swords should cut strongly. Spears and halberds must stand up to heavy use, bows and guns must be sturdy. Weapons should be hardy rather than decorative. You should not have a favourite weapon. To become over-familiar with one weapon is as much a fault as not knowing it sufficiently well. You should not copy others, but use weapons which you can handle properly. It is bad for commanders and troopers to have likes and dislikes. These are things you must learn thoroughly. Timing in Strategy There is timing in everything. Timing in strategy cannot be mastered without a great deal of practice. Timing is important in dancing and pipe or string music, for they are in rhythm only if timing is good. Timing and rhythm are also involved in the military arts, shooting bows and guns, and riding horses. In all skills and abilities there is timing. There is also timing in the Void. There is timing in the whole life of the warrior, in his thriving and declining, in his harmony and discord. Similarly, there is timing in the Way 10 of the merchant, in the rise and fall of capital. All things entail rising and falling timing. You must be able to discern this. In strategy there are various timing considerations. From the outset you must know the applicable timing and the inapplicable timing, and from among the large and small things and the fast and slow timings find the relevant timing, first seeing the distance timing and the background timing. This is the main thing in strategy. It is especially important to know the background timing, otherwise your strategy will become uncertain. You win battles with the timing in the Void born of the timing of cunning by knowing the enemies' timing, and thus using a timing which the enemy does not expect. All the five books are chiefly concerned with timing. You must train sufficiently to appreciate this. If you practice day and night in the above Ichi school strategy, your spirit will naturally broaden. Thus is large scale strategy and the strategy of hand to hand combat propagated in the world. This is recorded for the first time in the five books of Ground, Water, Fire, Tradition (Wind), and Void. This is the way for men who want to learn my strategy: 1. Do not think dishonestly. 2. The Way is in training. 3. Become acquainted with every art. 4. Know the Ways of all professions. 5. Distinguish between gain and loss in worldly matters. 6. Develop intuitive judgement and understanding for everything. 7. Perceive those things which cannot be seen. 8. Pay attention even to trifles. 9. Do nothing which is of no use. It is important to start by setting these broad principles in your heart, and train in the Way of Strategy. If you do not look at things on a large scale it will be difficult for you to master strategy. If you learn and attain this strategy you will never lose even to twenty or thirty enemies. More than anything to start with you must set your heart on strategy and earnestly stick to the Way. You will come to be able to actually beat men in fights, and to be able to win with your eye. Also by training you will be able to freely control your own body, conquer men with your body, and with sufficient training you will be able to beat ten men with your spirit. When you have reached this point, will it not mean that you are invincible? 11 Moreover, in large scale strategy the superior man will manage many subordinates dextrously, bear himself correctly, govern the country and foster the people, thus preserving the ruler's discipline. If there is a Way involving the spirit of not being defeated, to help oneself and gain honour, it is the Way of strategy.

CHAPTER 2

THE WATER BOOK

The spirit of the Ni Ten Ichi school of strategy is based on water, and this Water Book explains methods of victory as the long-sword form of the Ichi school. Language does not extend to explaining the Way in detail, but it can be grasped intuitively. Study this book; read a word then ponder on it. If you interpret the meaning loosely you will mistake the Way. The principles of strategy are written down here in terms of single combat, but you must think broadly so that you attain an understanding for ten-thousand-a-side battles. Strategy is different from other things in that if you mistake the Way even a little you will become bewildered and fall into bad ways. If you merely read this book you will not reach the Way of Strategy. Absorb the things written in this book.Do not just read, memorise or imitate, but so that you realize the principle from within your own heart study hard to absorb these things into your body. Spiritual Bearing in Strategy In strategy your spiritual bearing must not be any different from normal. Both in fighting and in everyday life you should be determined though calm. Meet the situation without tenseness yet not recklessly, your spirit settled yet unbiased. Even when your spirit is calm do not let your body relax, and when your body is relaxed do not let your spirit slacken. Do not let your spirit be influenced by your body, or your body be influenced by your spirit. Be neither insufficiently spirited nor over spirited. An elevated spirit is weak and a low spirit is weak. Do not let the enemy see your spirit. Small people must be completely familiar with the spirit of large people, and large people must be familiar with the spirit of small people. Whatever your size, do not be misled by the reactions of your own body. With your spirit open and unconstricted, look at things from a high point of view. You must cultivate your wisdom and spirit. Polish your 13 wisdom: learn public justice, distinguish between good and evil, study the Ways of different arts one by one. When you cannot be deceived by men you will have realized the wisdom of strategy. The wisdom of strategy is different from other things. On the battlefield, even when you are hard-pressed, you should ceaselessly research the principles of strategy so that you can develop a steady spirit. Stance in Strategy Adopt a stance with the head erect, neither hanging down, nor looking up, nor twisted. Your forehead and the space between your eyes should not be wrinkled. Do not roll your eyes nor allow them to blink, but slightly narrow them. With your features composed, keep the line of your nose straight with a feeling of slightly flaring your nostrils. Hold the line of the rear of the neck straight: instill vigour into your hairline, and in the same way from the shoulders down through your entire body. Lower both shoulders and, without the buttocks jutting out, put strength into your legs from the knees to the tips of your toes. Brace your abdomen so that you do not bend at the hips. Wedge your companion sword in your belt against your

21

abdomen, so that your belt is not slack - this is called "wedging in". In all forms of strategy, it is necessary to maintain the combat stance in everyday life and to make your everyday stance your combat stance. You must research this well. The Gaze in Strategy The gaze should be large and broad. This is the twofold gaze "Perception and Sight". Perception is strong and sight week. In strategy it is important to see distant things as if they were close and to take a distanced view of close things. It is important in strategy to know the enemy's sword and not to be distracted by insignificant movements of his sword. You must study this. The gaze is the same for single combat and for large-scale strategy. It is necessary in strategy to be able to look to both sides without moving the eyeballs. You cannot master this ability quickly. Learn what is written here; use this gaze in everyday life and do not vary it whatever happens. Holding the Long Sword 14 Grip the long sword with a rather floating feeling in your thumb and forefinger, with the middle finger neither tight nor slack, and with the last two fingers tight. It is bad to have play in your hands. When you take up a sword, you must feel intent on cutting the enemy. As you cut an enemy you must not change your grip, and your hands must not "cower". When you dash the enemy's sword aside, or ward it off, or force it down, you must slightly change the feeling in your thumb and forefinger. Above all, you must be intent on cutting the enemy in the way you grip the sword. The grip for combat and for sword-testing is the same. There is no such thing as a "man-cutting grip". Generally, I dislike fixedness in both long swords and hands. Fixedness means a dead hand. Pliability is a living hand. You must bear this in mind. Footwork With the tips of your toes somewhat floating, tread firmly with your heels. Whether you move fast or slow, with large or small steps, your feet must always move as in normal walking. I dislike the three walking methods know as "jumping-foot", "floating-foot" and "fixed-steps". So-called "Yin-Yang foot" is important in the Way. Yin-Yang foot means not moving only one foot. It means moving your feet left-right and right-left when cutting, withdrawing, or warding off a cut. You should not move on one foot preferentially. The Five Attitudes The five attitudes are: Upper, Middle, Lower, Right Side, and Left Side. These are the give. Although attitude has these five divisions, the one purpose of all of them is to cut the enemy. There are none but these five attitudes. Whatever attitude you are in, do not be conscious of making the attitude; think only of cutting. Your attitude should be large or small according to the situation. Upper, Lower and Middle attitudes are decisive. Left Side and Right Side attitudes are fluid. Left and Right attitudes should be used if there is an obstruction overhead or to one side. The decision to use Left or Right depends on the place. The essence of the Way is this. To understand attitude you must thoroughly understand the middle attitude. The middle attitude is the heart of attitudes. If we look at strategy on a broad scale, the Middle attitude is 15 the seat of the commander, with the other four attitudes following the commander. You must appreciate this. The Way of the Long Sword Knowing the Way of the long sword means we can wield with two fingers the sword we usually carry. If we know the path of the sword well, we can wield it easily. If you try to wield the long sword quickly you will mistake the Way. To wield the long sword well you must wield it calmly. If you try to wield it quickly, like a folding fan or a short sword, you will err by using "short sword chopping". You cannot cut down a man with a long sword using this method. When you have cut downwards with the longsword, lift it straight upwards; when you cut sideways, return the sword along a sideways path. Return the sword in a reasonable way, always stretching the elbows broadly. Wield the sword strongly. This is the Way of the longsword. If you learn to use the five approaches of my strategy, you will be able to wield a sword well. You must train constantly. The Five Approaches 1. The first approach is the Middle attitude. Confront the enemy with the point of your sword against his face. When he attacks, dash his sword to the right and "ride" it. Or, when the enemy attacks, deflect the point of his sword by hitting downwards, keep your long sword where it is, and as the enemy renews his attack cut his arms from below. This is the first method. The five approaches are this kind of thing. You must train repeatedly using a long sword in order to learn them. When you master my Way of the long sword, you will be able to control any attack the enemy makes. I assure you, there are no attitudes other than the five attitudes of the long sword of Ni To. 2. In the second approach with the long sword, from the Upper attitude cut the enemy just as he attacks. If the enemy evades the cut, keep your sword where it is and, scooping up from below, cut him as he renews the attack. It is possible to repeat the cut from here. In this method there are various changes in timing and spirit. You will be able to understand this by training in the Ichi school. You will always win with the five long sword methods. You must train repetitively. 3. In the third approach, adopt the Lower attitude, anticipating scooping up. When the enemy attacks, hit his hands from below. As you do so 16 he may try to hit your sword down. If this is the case, cut his upper arm(s) horizontally with a feeling of "crossing". This means that from the lower attitudes you hit the enemy at the instant that he attacks. You will encounter this method often, both as a beginner and in later strategy. You must train holding a long sword. 4. In this fourth approach, adopt the Left Side attitude. As the enemy attacks hit his hands from below. If as you hit his hands he attempts to dash down your sword, with the feeling of hitting his hands, parry the path of his long sword and cut across from above your shoulder. This is the Way of the long sword. Through this method you win by parrying the line of the enemy's attack. You must research this. 5. In the fifth approach, the sword is in the Right Side attitude. In accordance with the enemy's attack, cross your long sword from below at the side to the Upper attitude. Then cut straight from above. This method is essential for knowing the Way of the long sword well. If you can use this method, you can freely wield a heavy long sword. I cannot describe in detail how to use these five approaches. You must become well acquainted with my "in harmony with the long sword" Way, learn large-scale timing, understand the enemy's long sword, and become used to the five approaches from the outset. You will always win by using these five methods, with various timing considerations discerning the enemy's spirit. You must consider all this carefully. The "Attitude No-Attitude" Teaching "Attitude No-Attitude" means that there is no need for what are know as long sword attitudes. Even so, attitudes exist as the five ways of holding the long sword. However you hold the sword it must be in such a way that it is easy to cut the enemy well, in accordance with the situation, the place, and your relation to the enemy. From the Upper attitude as your spirit lessens you can adopt the Middle attitude, and from the Middle attitude you can raise the sword a little in your technique and adopt the Upper attitude. From the lower attitude you can raise the sword and adopt the Middle attitudes as the occasion demands. According to the situation, if you turn your sword from either the Left Side or Right Side attitude towards the centre, the Middle or the Lower attitude results. The principle of this is called "Existing Attitude - Nonexisting Attitude". The primary thing when you take a sword in your hands is your intention to cut the enemy, whatever the means. Whenever you parry, hit, 17 spring, strike or touch the enemy's cutting sword, you must cut the enemy in the same movement. It is essential to attain this. If you think only of hitting, springing, striking or touching the enemy, you will not be able actually to cut him. More than anything, you must be thinking of carrying your movement through to cutting him. You must thoroughly research this. Attitude in strategy on a larger scale is called "Battle Array". Such attitudes are all for winning battles. Fixed formation is bad. Study this well. To Hit the Enemy "In One Timing" "In One Timing" means, when you have closed with the enemy, to hit him as quickly and directly as possible, without moving your body or settling your spirit, while you see that he is still undecided. The timing of hitting before the enemy decides to withdraw, break or hit, is this "In One Timing". You must train to achieve this timing, to be able to hit in the timing of an instant. The "Abdomen Timing of Two" When you attack and the enemy quickly retreats, as you see him tense you must feint a cut. Then, as he relaxes, follow up and hit him. This is the "Abdomen Timing of Two". It is very difficult to attain this by merely reading this book, but you will soon understand with a little instruction. No Design, No Conception In this method, when the enemy attacks and you also decide to attack, hit with your body, and hit with your spirit, and hit from the Void with your hands, accelerating strongly. This is the "No Design, No Conception" cut. This is the most important method of hitting. It is often used. You must train hard to understand it. The Flowing Water Cut The "Flowing Water Cut" is used when you are struggling blade to blade with the enemy. When he breaks and quickly withdraws trying to spring with his long sword, expand your body and spirit and cut him as slowly as possible with your long sword, following your body like stagnant water. You can cut with certainty if you learn this. You must discern the enemy's grade. 18 Continuous Cut When you attack and the enemy also attacks, and your swords spring together, in one action cut his head, hands and legs. When you cut several places with one sweep of the long sword, it is the "Continuous Cut". You must practice this cut; it is often used. With detailed practice you should be able to understand it. The Fire and Stones Cut The Fires and Stones Cut means that when the enemy's long sword and your long sword clash together you cut as strongly as possible without raising the sword even a little. This means cutting quickly with the hands, body and legs - all three cutting strongly. If you train well enough you will be able to strike strongly. The Red Leaves Cut The Red Leaves Cut [allusion to falling, dying leaves] means knocking down the enemy's long sword. The spirit should be getting control of his sword. When the enemy is in a long sword attitude in front of you and intent on cutting, hitting and parrying, you strongly hit the enemy's long sword with the Fire and Stones Cut, perhaps in the spirit of the "No Design, No Conception" Cut. If you then beat down the point of his sword with a sticky feeling, he will necessarily drop the sword. If you practice this cut it becomes easy to make the enemy drop his sword. You must train repetitively. The Body in Place of the Long

Sword Also "the long sword in place of the body". Usually we move the body and the sword at the same time to cut the enemy. However, according to the enemy's cutting method, you can dash against him with your body first, and afterwards cut with the sword. If his body is immoveable, you can cut first with the long sword, but generally you hit first with the body and then cut with the long sword. You must research this well and practice hitting. Cut and Slash To cut and to slash are two different things. Cutting, whatever form of cutting it is, is decisive, with a resolute spirit. Slashing is nothing more than touching the enemy. Even if you slash strongly, and even if the enemy dies instantly, it is slashing. When you cut, your spirit is resolved. 19 You must appreciate this. If you first slash the enemy's hands or legs, you must then cut strongly. Slashing is in spirit the same as touching. When you realize this, they become indistinguishable. Learn this well. Chinese Monkey's Body The Chinese Monkey's Body is the spirit of not stretching out your arms. The spirit is to get in quickly, without in the least extending your arms, before the enemy cuts. If you are intent upon not stretching out your arms you are effectively far away, the spirit is to go in with your whole body. When you come to within arm's reach it becomes easy to move your body in. You must research this well. Glue and Lacquer Emulsion Body The spirit of "Glue and Lacquer Emulsion Body" is to stick to the enemy and not separate from him. When you approach the enemy, stick firmly with your head, body and legs. People tend to advance their head and legs quickly, but their body lags behind. You should stick firmly so that there is not the slightest gap between the enemy's body and your body. You must consider this carefully. To Strive for Height By "to strive for height" is meant, when you close with the enemy, to strive with him for superior height without cringing. Stretch your legs, stretch your hips, and stretch your neck face to face with him. When you think you have won, and you are the higher, thrust in strongly. You must learn this. To Apply Stickiness When the enemy attacks and you also attack with the long sword, you should go in with a sticky feeling and fix your long sword against the enemy's as you receive his cut. The spirit of stickiness is not hitting very strongly, but hitting so that the long swords do not separate easily. It is best to approach as calmly as possible when hitting the enemy's long sword with stickiness. The difference between "Stickiness" and "Entanglement" is that stickiness is firm and entanglement is weak. You must appreciate this. The Body Strike The Body Strike means to approach the enemy through a gap in his guard. The spirit is to strike him with your body. Turn your face a little 20 aside and strike the enemy's breast with your left shoulder thrust out. Approach with the spirit of bouncing the enemy away, striking as strongly as possible in time with yout breathing. If you achieve this method of closing with the enemy, you will be able to knock him ten or twenty feet away. It is possible to strike the enemy until he is dead. Train well. Three Ways to Parry His Attack There are three methods to parry a cut: First, by dashing the enemy's long sword to your right, as if thrusting at his eyes, when he makes an attack. Or, to parry by thrusting the enemy's long sword towards his right eye with the feeling of snipping his neck. Or, when you have a short "long sword", without worrying about parrying the enemy's long sword, to close with him quickly, thrusting at his face with your left hand. These are the three methods of parrying. You must bear in mind that you can always clench your left hand and thrust at the enemy's face with your fist. For this it is necessary to train well. To Stab at the Face To stab at the face means, when you are in confrontation with the enemy, that your spirit is intent of stabbing at his face, following the line of the blades with the point of your long sword. If you are intent on stabbing at his face, his face and body will become rideable. When the enemy becomes as if rideable, there are various opportunities for winning. You must concentrate on this. When fighting and the enemy's body becomes as if rideable, you can win quickly, so you ought not to forget to stab at the face. You must pursue the value of this technique through training. To Stab at the Heart To stab at the heart means, when fighting and there are obstructions above, or to the sides, and whenever it is difficult to cut, to thrust at the enemy. You must stab the enemy's breast without letting the point of your long sword waver, showing the enemy the ridge of the blade square-on, and with the spirit of deflecting his long sword. The spirit of this principle is often useful when we become tired or for some reason our long

31

sword will not cut. You must understand the application of this method. 21 To Scold "Tut-TUT!" "Scold" means that, when the enemy tries to counter-cut as you attack, you counter-cut again from below as if thrusting at him, trying to hold him down. With very quick timing you cut, scolding the enemy. Thrust up, "Tut!", and cut "TUT!" This timing is encountered time and time again in exchange of blows. The way to scold Tut-TUT is to time the cut simultaneously with raising your long sword as if to thrust the enemy. You must learn this through repetitive practice. The Smacking Parry By "smacking parry" is meant that when you clash swords with the enemy, you meet his attacking cut on your long sword with a tee-dum, teedum rhythm, smacking his sword and cutting him. The spirit of the smacking parry is not parrying, or smacking strongly, but smacking the enemy's long sword in accordance with his attacking cut, primarily intent on quickly cutting him. If you understand the timing of smacking, however hard your long swords clash together, your swordpoint will not be knocked back even a little. You must research sufficiently to realize this. There are Many Enemies "There are many enemies" applies when you are fighting one against many. Draw both sword and companion sword and assume a widestretched left and right attitude. The spirit is to chase the enemies around from side to side, even though they come from all four directions. Observe their attacking order, and go to meet first those who attack first. Sweep your eyes around broadly, carefully examining the attacking order, and cut left and right alternately with your swords. Waiting is bad. Always quickly re-assume your attitudes to both sides, cut the enemies down as they advance, crushing them in the direction from which they attack. Whatever you do, you must drive the enemy together, as if tying a line of fishes, and when they are seen to be piled up, cut them down strongly without giving them room to move. The Advantage when Coming to Blows You can know how to win through strategy with the long sword, but it cannot be clearly explained in writing. You must practice diligently in order to understand how to win. 22 Oral tradition: "The true Way of Strategy is revealed in the long sword." One Cut You can win with certainty with the spirit of "one cut". It is difficult to attain this if you do not learn strategy well. If you train well in this Way, strategy will come from your heart and you will be able to win at will. You must train diligently. Direct Communication The spirit of "Direct Communication" is how the true Way of the Ni To Ichi school is received and handed down. Oral tradition: "Teach your body strategy." Recorded in the above book is an outline of Ichi school sword-fighting. To learn how to win with the long sword in strategy, first learn the five approaches and the five attitudes, and absorb the Way of the long sword naturally in your body. You must understand spirit and timing, handle the long sword naturally, and move body and legs in harmony with your spirit. Whether beating one man or two, you will then know values in strategy. Study the contents of this book, taking one item at a time, and through fighting with enemies you will gradually come to know the principle of the Way. Deliberately, with a patient spirit, absorb the virtue of all this, from time to time raising your hand in combat. Maintain this spirit whenever you cross swords with and enemy. Step by step walk the thousand-mile road. Study strategy over the years and achieve the spirit of the warrior. Today is victory over yourself of yesterday; tomorrow is your victory over lesser men. Next, in order to beat more skillful men, train according to this book, not allowing your heart to be swayed along a side-track. Even if you kill an enemy, if it is not based on what you have learned it is not the true Way. If you attain this Way of victory, then you will be able to beat several tens of men. What remains is sword-fighting ability, which you can attain in battles and duels.

CHAPTER 3

THE FIRE BOOK

In this the Fire Book of the Ni To Ichi school of strategy I describe fighting as fire. In the first place, people think narrowly about the benefit of strategy. By using only their fingertips, they only know the benefit of three of the five inches of the wrist. They let a contest be decided, as with the folding fan, merely by the span of their forearms. They specialise in the small matter of dexterity, learning such trifles as hand and leg movements with the bamboo practice sword. In my strategy, the training for killing enemies is by way of many contests, fighting for survival, discovering the meaning of life and death, learning the Way of the sword, judging the strength of attacks and understanding the Way of the "edge and ridge" of the sword. You cannot profit from small techniques particularly when full armour is worn. My Way of Strategy is the sure method to win when fighting for your life one man against five or ten. There is nothing wrong with the principle "one man can beat ten, so a thousand men can beat ten thousand". You must research this. Of course you cannot assemble a thousand or ten thousand men for everyday training. But you can become a master of strategy by training alone with a sword, so that you can understand the enemy's strategy, his strength and resources, and come to appreciate how to apply strategy to beat ten thousand enemies. Any man who wants to master the essence of my strategy must research diligently, training morning and evening. Thus can he polish his skill, become free from self, and realize extraordinary ability. He will come to possess miraculous power. This is the practical result of strategy. Depending on the Place Examine your environment. 24 Stand in the sun; that is, take up an attitude with the sun behind you. If the situation does not allow this, you must try to keep the sun on your right side. In buildings, you must stand with the entrance behind you or to your right. Make sure that your rear is unobstructed, and that there is free space on your left, your right side being occupied with your side attitude. At night, if the enemy can be seen, keep the fire behind you and the entrance to your right, and otherwise take up your attitude as above. You must look down on the enemy, and take up your attitude on slightly higher places. For example, the Kamiza in a house is thought of as a high place. When the fight comes, always endeavour to chase the enemy around to your left side. Chase him towards awkward places, and try to keep him with his back to awkward places. When the enemy gets into an inconvenient position, do not let him look around, but conscientiously chase him around and pin him down. In houses, chase the enemy into the thresholds, lintels, doors, verandas, pillars, and so on, again not letting him see his situation. Always chase the enemy into bad footholds, obstacles at the side, and so on, using the virtues of the place to establish predominant positions from which to fight. You must research and train diligently in this. The Three Methods to Forestall the Enemy The first is to forestall him by attacking. This is called Ken No Sen (to set him up). Another method is to forestall him as he attacks. This is called Tai No Sen (to wait for the initiative). The other method is when you and the enemy attack together. This is called Tai Tai No Sen (to accompany him and forestall him). There are no methods of taking the lead other than these three. Because you can win quickly by taking the lead, it is one of the most important things in strategy. There are several things involved in taking the lead. You must make the best of the situation, see through the enemy's spirit so that you grasp his strategy and defeat him. It is impossible to write about this in detail. The First - Ken No Sen When you decide to attack, keep calm and dash in quickly, forestalling the enemy. Or you can advance seemingly strongly but with a reserved spirit, forestalling him with the reserve. 25 Alternatively, advance with as strong a spirit as possible, and when you reach the enemy move with your feet a little quicker than normal, unsettling him and overwhelming him sharply. Or, with your spirit calm, attack with a feeling of constantly crushing the enemy, from first to last. The spirit is to win in the depths of the enemy. These are all Ken No Sen. The Second - Tai No Sen When the enemy attacks, remain undisturbed but feign weakness. As the enemy reaches you, suddenly move away indicating that you intend to jump aside, then dash in attacking strongly as soon as you see the enemy relax. This is one way. Or, as the enemy attacks, attack still more strongly, taking advantage of the resulting disorder in his timing to win. This is the Tai No Sen principle. The Third - Tai Tai No Sen When the enemy makes a quick attack, you must attack strongly and calmly, aim for his weak point as he draws near, and strongly defeat him. Or, if the enemy attacks calmly, you must observe his movements and, with your body rather floating, join in with his movements as he draws near. Move quickly and cut him strongly. This is Tai Tai No Sen. These things cannot be clearly explained in words. You must research what is written here. In these three ways of forestalling, you must judge the situation. This does not mean that you always attack first; but if the enemy attacks first you can lead him around. In strategy, you have effectively won when you forestall the enemy, so you must train well to attain this. To Hold Down a Pillow "To Hold Down a Pillow" means not allowing the enemy's head to rise. In contests of strategy it is bad to be led about by the enemy. You must always be able to lead the enemy about. Obviously the enemy will also be thinking of doing this, but he cannot forestall you if you do not allow him to come out. In strategy, you must stop the enemy as he attempts to cut; you must push down his thrust, and throw off his hold when he tries to grapple. This is the meaning of "to hold down a pillow". When you have grasped this principle, whatever the enemy tries to bring about in the fight you will see in advance and suppress it. The spirit is too 26 check his attack at the syllable "at... ", when he jumps check his jump at the syllable "ju... ", and check his cut at "cu... ". The important thing in strategy is to suppress the enemy's useful actions but allow his useless actions. However, doing this alone is defensive. First, you must act according to the Way, suppressing the enemy's techniques, foiling his plans and thence command him directly. When you can do this you will be a master of strategy. You must train well and research "holding down a pillow". Crossing at a Ford "Crossing at a ford" means, for example, crossing the sea at a strait, or crossing over a hundred miles of broad sea at a crossing place. I believe this "crossing at a ford" occurs often in man's lifetime. It means setting sail even though your friends stay in harbour, knowing the route, knowing the soundness of your ship and the favour of the day. When all the conditions are meet, and there is perhaps a favourable wind, or a tailwind, then set sail. If the wind changes within a few miles of your destination, you must row across the remaining distance without sail. If you attain this spirit, it applies to everyday life. You must always think of crossing at a ford. In strategy also it is important to "cross at a ford". Discern the enemy's capability and, knowing your own strong points, "cross the ford" at the advantageous place, as a good captain crosses a sea route. If you succeed in crossing at the best place, you may take your ease. To cross at a ford means to attack the enemy's weak point, and to put yourself in an advantageous position. This is how to win large-scale strategy. The spirit of crossing at a ford is necessary in both large- and small-scale strategy. You must research this well. To Know the Times "To know the times" means to know the enemy's disposition in battle. Is it flourishing or waning? By observing the spirit of the enemy's men and getting the best position, you can work out the enemy's disposition and move your men accordingly. You can win through this principle of strategy, fighting from a position of advantage. When in a duel, you must forestall the enemy and attack when you have first recognised his school of strategy, perceived his quality and his strong and weak points. Attack in an unsuspecting manner, knowing his metre and modulation and the appropriate timing. 27 Knowing the times means, if your ability is high, seeing right into things. If you are thoroughly conversant with strategy, you will recognise the enemy's intentions and thus have many opportunities to win. You must sufficiently study this. To Tread Down the Sword "To tread down the sword" is a principle often used in strategy. First, in large scale strategy, when the enemy first discharges bows and guns and then attacks it is difficult for us to attack if we are busy loading powder into our guns or notching our arrows. The spirit is to attack quickly while the enemy is still shooting with bows or guns. The spirit is to win by "treading down" as we receive the enemy's attack. In single combat, we cannot get a decisive victory by cutting, with a "tee-dum tee-dum" feeling, in the wake of the enemy's attacking long sword. We must defeat him at the start of his attack, in the spirit of treading him down with the feet, so that he cannot rise again to the attack. "Treading" does not simply mean treading with the feet. Tread with the body, tread with the spirit, and, of course, tread and cut with the long sword. You must achieve the spirit of not allowing the enemy to attack a second time. This is the spirit of forestalling in every sense. Once at the enemy, you should not aspire just to strike him, but to cling after the attack. You must study this deeply. To Know "Collapse" Everything can collapse. Houses, bodies, and enemies collapse when their rhythm becomes deranged. In large-scale strategy, when the enemy starts to collapse, you must pursue him without letting the chance go. If you fail to take advantage of your enemies' collapse, they may recover. In single combat, the enemy sometimes loses timing and collapses. If you let this opportunity pass, he may recover and not be so negligent thereafter. Fix your eye on the enemy's collapse, and chase him, attacking so that you do not let him recover. You must do this. The chasing attack is with a strong spirit. You must utterly cut the enemy down so that he does not recover his position. You must understand how to utterly cut down the enemy. To Become the Enemy "To become the enemy" means to think yourself in the enemy's position. In the world people tend to think of a robber trapped in a house as 28 a fortified enemy. However, if we think of "becoming the enemy", we feel that the whole world is against us and that there is no escape. He who is shut inside is a pheasant. He who enters to arrest is a hawk. You must appreciate this. In large-scale strategy, people are always under the impression that the enemy is strong, and so tend to become cautious. But if you have good soldiers, and if you understand the principles of strategy, and if you know how to beat the enemy, there is nothing to worry about. In single combat also you must put yourself in the enemy's position. If you think, "Here is a a master of the Way, who knows the principles of strategy", then you will surely lose. You must consider this deeply. To Release Four Hands "To release four hands" is used when you and the enemy are contending with the same spirit, and the issue cannot be decided. Abandon this spirit and win through an alternative resource. In large-scale strategy, when there is a "four hands" spirit, do not give up - it is man's existence. Immediately throw away this spirit and win with a technique the enemy does not expect. In single combat also, when we think we have fallen into the "four hands" situation, we must defeat the enemy by changing our mind and applying a suitable technique according to his condition. You must be able to judge this. To Move the Shade "To move the shade" is used when you cannot see the enemy's spirit. In large-scale strategy, when you cannot see the enemy's position, indicate that you are about to attack strongly, to discover his resources. It is easy then to defeat him with a different method once you see his resources. In single combat, if the enemy takes up a rear or side attitude of the long sword so that you cannot see his intention, make a feint attack, and the enemy will show his long sword, thinking he sees your spirit. Benefiting from what you are shown, you can win with certainty. If you are negligent you will miss the timing. Research this well. To Hold Down a Shadow "Holding down a shadow" is use when you can see the enemy's attacking spirit. 29 In large-scale strategy, when the enemy embarks on an attack, if you make a show of strongly suppressing his technique, he will change his mind. Then, altering your spirit, defeat him by forestalling him with a Void spirit. Or, in single combat, hold down the enemy's strong intention with a suitable timing, and defeat him by forestalling him with this timing. You must study this well. To Pass On Many things are said to be passed on. Sleepiness can be passed on, and yawning can be passed on. Time can be passed on also. In large-scale strategy, when the enemy is agitated and shows an inclination to rush, do not mind in the least. Make a show of complete calmness, and the enemy will be taken by this and will become relaxed. When you see that this spirit has been passed on, you can bring about the enemy's defeat by attacking strongly with a Void spirit. In single combat, you can win by relaxing your body and spirit and then, catching on to the moment the enemy relaxes, attack strongly and quickly, forestalling him. What is know as "getting someone drunk" is similar to this. You can also infect the enemy with a bored, careless, or weak spirit. You must study this well. To Cause Loss of Balance Many things can cause a loss of balance. One cause is danger, another is hardship, and another is surprise. You must research this. In large-scale strategy it is important to cause loss of balance. Attack without warning where the enemy is

THE BOOK OF FIVE RINGS

not expecting it, and while his spirit is undecided follow up your advantage and, having the lead, defeat him. Or, in single combat, start by making a show of being slow, then suddenly attack strongly. Without allowing him space for breath to recover form the fluctuation of spirit, you must grasp the opportunity to win. Get the feel of this. To Frighten Fright often occurs, caused by the unexpected. In large-scale strategy you can frighten the enemy not just by what you present to their eyes, but by shouting, making a small force seem large, or by threatening them from the flank without warning. These 30 things all frighten. You can win by making best use of the enemy's frightened rhythm. In single combat, also, you must use the advantage of taking the enemy unawares by frightening him with your body, long sword, or voice, to defeat him. You should research this well. To Soak In When you have come to grips and are striving together with the enemy, and you realize that you cannot advance, you "soak in" and become one with the enemy. You can win by applying a suitable technique while you are mutually entangled. In battles involving large numbers as well as in fights with small numbers, you can often win decisively with the advantage of knowing how to "soak" into the enemy, whereas, were you to draw apart, you would lose the chance to win. Research this well. To Injure the Corners It is difficult to move strong things by pushing directly, so you should "injure the corners". In large-scale strategy, it is beneficial to strike at the corners of the enemy's force. If the corners are overthrown, the spirit

of the whole body will be overthrown. To defeat the
enemy you must follow up the attack when the corners
have fallen. In single combat, it is easy to win once the
enemy collapses. This happens when you injure the
"corners" of his body, and thus weaken him. It is
important to know how to do this, so you must research
deeply. To Throw into Confusion This means making the
enemy lose resolve. In large-scale strategy we can use
our troops to confuse the enemy on the field. Observing
the enemy's spirit, we can make him think, "Here?
There? Like that? Like this? Slow? Fast?". Victory is
certain when the enemy is caught up in a rhythm which
confuses his spirit. In single combat, we can confuse the
enemy by attacking with varied techniques when the
chance arises. Feint a thrust or cut, or make the enemy
think ou are going to close with him, and when he is
confused you can easily win. This is the essence of
fighting, and you must research it deeply. The Three
Shouts 31 The three shouts are divided thus: before,
during and after. Shout according to the situation. The
voice is a thing of life. We shout against fires and so on,
against the wind and the waves. The voice shows
energy. In large-scale strategy, at the start of battle we
shout as loudly as possible. During the fight, the voice is
low-pitched, shouting out as we attack. After the
contest, we shout in the wake of our victory. These are
the three shouts. In single combat, we make as if to cut
and shout "Ei!" at the same time to disturb the enemy,
then in the wake of our shout we cut with the long
sword. We shout after we have cut down the enemy -

this is to announce victory. This is called "sen go no koe" (before and after voice). We do not shout simultaneously with flourishing the long sword. We shout during the fight to get into rhythm. Research this deeply. To Mingle In battles, when the armies are in confrontation, attack the enemy's strong points and, when you see that they are beaten back, quickly separate and attack yet another strong point on the periphery of his force. The spirit of this is like a winding mountain path. This is an important fighting method for one man against many. Strike down the enemies in one quarter, or drive them back, then grasp the timing and attack further strong points to right and left, as if on a winding mountain path, weighing up the enemies' disposition. When you know the enemies' level attack strongly with no trace of retreating spirit. What is meant by "mingling" is the spirit of advancing and becoming engaged with the enemy, and not withdrawing even one step. You must understand this. To Crush This means to crush the enemy regarding him as being weak. In large-scale strategy, when we see that the enemy has few men, or if he has many men but his spirit is weak and disordered, we knock the hat over his eyes, crushing him utterly. If we crush lightly, he may recover. You must learn the spirit of crushing as if with a hand-grip. In single combat, if the enemy is less skilful than ourself, if his rhythm is disorganised, or if he has fallen into evasive or retreating attitudes, we must crush him straightaway, with no concern for his presence and without allowing him space for breath. It is essential to crush him all at once. The primary thing is not to let him recover his position even a little. You must research this deeply. 32 The Mountain-Sea Change The "mountain-sea" spirit means that it is bad to repeat the same thing several times when fighting the enemy. There may be no help but to do something twice, but do not try it a third time. If you once make an attack and fail, there is little chance of success if you use the same approach again. If you attempt a technique which you have previously tried unsuccessfully and fail yet again, then you must change your attacking method. If the enemy thinks of the mountains, attack like the sea; and if he thinks of the sea, attack like the mountains. You must research this deeply. To Penetrate the Depths When we are fighting with the enemy, even when it can be seen that we can win on the surface with the benefit of the Way, if his spirit is not extinguished, he may be beaten superficially yet undefeated in spirit deep inside. With this principle of "penetrating the depths" we can destroy the enemy's spirit in its depths, demoralising him by quickly changing our spirit. This often occurs. Penetrating the depths means penetrating with the long sword, penetrating with the body, and penetrating with the spirit. This cannot be understood in a generalisation. Once we have crushed the enemy in the depths, there is no need to remain spirited. But otherwise we must remain spirited. If the enemy remains spirited it is difficult to crush him. You must train in penetrating the depths for large-scale strategy and also single combat. To Renew "To renew" applies when we are fighting with the enemy, and an entangled spirit arises where there is no possible resolution. We must abandon our efforts, think of the situation in a fresh spirit then win in the new rhythm. To renew, when we are deadlocked with the enemy, means that without changing our circumstance we change our spirit and win through a different technique. It is necessary to consider how "to renew" also applies in large-scale strategy. Research this diligently. Rat's Head, Ox's Neck 33 "Rat's head and ox's neck" means that, when we are fighting with the enemy and both he and we have become occupied with small points in an entangled spirit, we must always think of the Way of Strategy as being both a rat's head and an ox's neck. Whenever we have become preoccupied with small detail, we must suddenly change into a large spirit, interchanging large with small. This is one of the essences of strategy. It is necessary that the warrior think in this spirit in everyday life. You must not depart from this spirit in large-scale strategy nor in single combat. The Commander Knows the Troops "The commander knows the troops" applies everywhere in fights in my Way of strategy. Using the wisdom of strategy, think of the enemy as your own troops. When you think in this way you can move him at will and be able to chase him around. You become the general and the enemy becomes your troops. You must master this. To Let Go the Hilt There are various kinds of spirit involved in letting go the hilt. There is the spirit of winning without a sword. There is also the spirit of holding the long sword but not winning. The various methods cannot be expressed in writing. You must train well. The Body of a Rock When you have mastered the Way of Strategy you can suddenly make your body like a rock, and ten thousand things cannot touch you. This is the body of a rock. You will not be moved. Oral tradition. What is recorded above is what has been constantly on my mind about Ichi school sword fencing, written down as it came to me. This is the first time I have written about my technique, and the order of things is a bit confused. It is difficult to express it clearly. This book is a spiritual guide for the man who wishes to learn the Way. My heart has been inclined to the Way of Strategy from my youth onwards. I have devoted myself to training my hand, tempering my body, and attaining the many spiritual attitudes of sword fencing. If we watch men of other schools discussing theory, and concentrating on techniques with the hands, even though they seem skilful to watch, they have not the slightest true spirit. 34 Of course, men who study in this way think they are training the body and spirit, but it is an obstacle to the true Way, and its bad influence remains for ever. Thus the true Way of Strategy is becoming decadent and dying out. The true Way ᴦ sword fencing is the craft of defeating the enemy ⁱ fight, and nothing other than this. If you attair adhere to the wisdom of my strategy, you neeᴦ doubt that you will win.

CHAPTER 4

THE WIND BOOK

In strategy you must know the Ways of other schools, so I have written about various other traditions of strategys in this the Wind Book. Without knowledge of the Ways of other schools, it is difficult to understand the essence of my Ichi school. Looking at other schools we find some that specialise in techniques of strength using extra-long swords. Some schools study the Way of the short sword, known as kodachi. Some schools teach dexterity in large numbers of sword techniques, teaching attitudes of the sword as the "surface" and the Way as the "interior". That none of these are the true Way I show clearly in the interior of this book - all the vices and virtues and rights and wrongs. My Ichi school is different. Other schools make accomplishments their means of livelihood, growing flowers and decoratively colouring articles in order to sell them. This is definitely not the Way of Strategy. Some of the world's strategists are concerned only with sword-fencing, and limit their training to flourishing the long sword and carriage of the body. But is dexterity alone sufficient to win? This is not the essence of the Way. I have recorded the unsatisfactory point of other schools one by one in this book. You must study these matters deeply to appreciate the benefit of my Ni To Ichi school. Other Schools Using Extra-Long Swords Some other schools have a liking for extra-long swords. From the point of 'iew of my strategy these must been seen as weak schools. This is because they do not appreciate the principle of cutting the enemy by any means. Their preference is for the extra-long sword and, relying on the virtue of its length, they think to defeat the enemy from a distance. In this world it is said, "One inch gives the hand advantage", but these are the idle words of one who does not know strategy. It shows the 36 inferior strategy of a weak spirit that men should be dependent on the length of their sword, fighting from a distance without the benefit of strategy. I expect there is a case for the school in question liking extra-long swords as part of its doctrine, but if we compare this to real life it is unreasonable. Surely we need not necessarily be defeated if we are using a short sword, and have no long sword? It is difficult for these people to cut the enemy when at close quarters because of the length of the long sword. The blade path is large so the long sword is an encumbrance, and they are at a disadvantage compared to the man armed with a short companion sword. From olden times it has been said: "Great and small go together.". So do not unconditionally dislike extra-long swords. What I dislike is the inclination towards the long sword. If we consider large-scale strategy, we can think of large forces in terms of long swords, and small forces as short swords. Cannot few me give battle against many? There are many instances of few men overcoming many. You' strategy is of no account if when called on to fight i confined space your heart is inclined to the long s' or if you are in a house armed only with your com sword. Besides, some men have not the strength of others. In my doctrine, I dislike preconceived, narrow spirit. You must study this well. The Strong Long Sword Spirit in Other Schools You should not speak of strong and weak long swords. If you just wield the long sword in a strong spirit your cutting will be coarse, and if you use the sword coarsely you will have difficulty in winning. If you are concerned with the strength of your sword, you will try to cut unreasonably strongly, and will not be able to cut at all. It is also bad to try to cut strongly when testing the sword. Whenever you cross swords with an enemy you must not think of cutting him either strongly or weakly; just think of cutting and killing him. Be intent solely upon killing the enemy. Do not try to cut strongly and, of course, do not think of cutting weakly. You should only be concerned with killing the enemy. If you rely on strength, when you hit the enemy's sword you will inevitably hit too hard. If you do this, your own sword will be carried along as a result. Thus the saying, "The strongest hand wins", has no meaning. In large-scale strategy, if you have a strong army and are relying on strength to win, but the enemy also has a strong army, the battle will be fierce. This is the same for both sides. 37 Without the correct principle the fight cannot be won. The spirit of my school is to win through the wisdom of strategy, paying no attention to trifles. Study this well. Use of the Shorter Long Sword in Other Schools Using a shorter long sword is not the true Way to win. In ancient times, tachi and katana meant long and short swords. Men of superior strength in the world can wield even a long sword lightly, so there is no case for their liking the short sword. They also make use of the length of spears and halberds. Some men use a shorter long sword with the intention of jumping in and stabbing the enemy at the unguarded moment when he flourishes his sword. This inclination is bad. To aim for the enemy's unguarded moment is completely defensive, and undesirable at close quarters with the enemy. Furthermore, you cannot use the method of jumping inside his defence with a short sword if there are many enemies. Some men think that if they go against many enemies with a shorter long sword they can unrestrictedly frisk around cutting in sweeps, but they have to parry cuts continuously, and eventually become entangled with the enemy. This is inconsistent with the true Way of Strategy. The sure Way to win thus is to chase the enemy around in confusing manner, causing him to jump aside, with your body held strongly and straight. The same principle applies to large-scale strategy. The essence of strategy is to fall upon the enemy in large numbers and bring about his speedy downfall. By their study of strategy, people of the world get used to countering, evading and retreating as the normal thing. They become set in this habit, so can easily be paraded around by the enemy. The Way of Strategy is straight and true. You must chase the enemy around and make him obey your spirit. Other Schools with many Methods of using the Long Sword Placing a great deal of importance on the attitudes of the long sword is a mistaken way of thinking. What is known in the world as "attitude" applies when there is no enemy. The reason is that this has been a precedent since ancient times, and there should be no such thing as "This is the modern way to do it" in dueling. You must force the enemy into inconvenient situations. Attitudes are for situations in which you are not to be moved. That is, for garrisoning castles, battle array, and so on, showing the spirit of not being moved even by a strong assault. In the Way of dueling, however, 38 you must always be intent upon taking the lead and attacking. Attitude is the spirit of awaiting an attack. You must appreciate this. In duels of strategy you must move the opponent's attitude. Attack where his spirit is lax, throw him into confusion, irritate and terrify him. Take advantage of the enemy's rhythm when he is unsettled and you can win. I dislike the defensive spirit know as "attitude". Therefore, in my Way, there is something called "Attitude-No Attitude". In large-scale strategy we deploy our troops for battle bearing in mind our strength, observing the enemy's numbers, and noting the details of the battle field. This is at the start of the battle. The spirit of attacking first is completely different from the spirit of being attacked. Bearing an attack well, with a strong attitude, and parrying the enemy's attack well, is like making a wall of spears and halberds. When you attack the enemy, your spirit must go to the extent of pulling the stakes out of a wall and using them as spears and halberds. You must examine this well. Fixing the Eyes in Other Schools Some schools maintain that the eyes should be fixed on the enemy's long sword. Some schools fix the eyes on the hands. Some fix the eyes on the face, and some fix the eyes on the feet, and so on. If you fix the eyes on these places your spirit can become confused and your strategy thwarted. I will explain this in detail. Footballers do not fix their eyes on the ball, but by good play on the field they can perform well. When you become accustomed to something, you are not limited to the use of your eyes. People such as master musicians have the music score in front of their nose, or flourish swords in several ways when they have mastered the Way, but this does not mean that they fix their eyes on these things specifically, or that they make pointless movements of the sword. It means that they can see naturally. In the Way of Strategy, when you have fought many times you will easily be able to appraise the speed and position of the enemy's sword, and having mastery of the Way you will see the weight of his spirit. In strategy, fixing the eyes means gazing at the man's heart. In large-scale strategy the area to watch is the enemy's strength. "Perception" and "sight" are the two methods of seeing. Perception consists of concentrating strongly on the enemy's spirit, observing the 39 condition of the battlefield, fixing the gaze strongly, seeing the progress of the fight and the changes of advantages. This is the sure way to win. In single combat you must not fix the eyes on the details. As I said before, if you fix your eyes on details and neglect important things, your spirit will become bewildered, and victory will escape you.

Research this principle well and train diligently. Use of the Feet in Other Schools There are various methods of using the feet: floating foot, jumping foot, springing foot, treading foot, crow's foot, and such nimble walking methods. From the point of view of my strategy, these are all unsatisfactory. I dislike floating foot because the feet always tend to float during the fight. The Way must be trod firmly. Neither do I like jumping foot, because it encourages the habit of jumping, and a jumpy spirit. However much you jump, there is no real justification for it; so jumping is bad. Springing foot causes a springing spirit which is indecisive. Treading foot is a "waiting" method, and I especially dislike it. Apart from these, there are various fast walking methods, such as crow's foot, and so on. Sometimes, however, you may encounter the enemy on marshland, swampy ground, river valleys, stony ground, or narrow roads, in which situations you cannot jump or move the feet quickly. In my strategy, the footwork does not change. I always walk as I usually do in the street. You must never lose control of your feet. According to the enemy's rhythm, move fast or slowly, adjusting you body not too much and not too little. Carrying the feet is important also in large-scale strategy. This is because, if you attack quickly and thoughtlessly without knowing the enemy's spirit, your rhythm will become deranged and you will not be able to win. Or, if you advance too slowly, you will not be able to take advantage of the enemy's disorder, the opportunity to win will escape, and you will not be able to finish the fight quickly. You must win by seizing upon the enemy's disorder and derangement, and by not according him even a little hope of recovery. Practice this well. Speed in Other Schools 40 Speed is not part of the true Way of Strategy. Speed implies that things seem fast or slow, according to whether or not they are in rhythm. Whatever the Way, the master of strategy does not appear fast. Some people can walk as fast as a hundred or a hundred and twenty miles in a day, but this does not mean that they run continuously from morning till night. Unpracticed runners may seem to have been running all day, but their performance is poor. In the Way of dance, accomplished performers can sing while dancing, but when beginners try this they slow down and their spirit becomes busy. The "old pine tree" melody beaten on a leather drum is tranquil, but when beginners try this they slow down and their spirit becomes busy. Very skilful people can manage a fast rhythm, but it is bad to beat hurriedly. If you try to beat too quickly you will get out of time. Of course, slowness is bad. Really skilful people never get out of time, and are always deliberate, and never appear busy. From this example, the principle can be seen. What is known as speed is especially bad in the Way of Strategy. The reason for this is that depending on the place, marsh or swamp and so on, it may not be possible to move the body and legs together quickly. Still less will you be able to cut quickly if you have a long sword in this situation. If you try to cut quickly, as if using a fan or short sword, you will not actually cut even a little. You must appreciate this. In large-scale strategy also, a fast busy spirit is undesirable. The spirit must be that of holding down a pillow, then you will not be even a little late. When your opponent is hurrying recklessly, you must act contrarily and keep calm. You must not be influenced by the opponent. Train diligently to attain this spirit. "Interior" and "Surface" in Other Schools There is no "interior" nor "surface" in strategy. The artistic accomplishments usually claim inner meaning and secret tradition, and "interior" and "gate", but in combat there is no such thing as fighting on the surface, or cutting with the interior. When I teach my Way, I first teach by training in techniques which are easy for the pupil to understand, a doctrine which is easy to understand. I gradually endeavour to explain the deep principle, points which it is hardly possible to comprehend, according to the pupil's progress. In any event, because the way to understanding is through experience, I do not speak of "interior" and "gate". 41 In this world, if you go into the mountains, and decide to go deeper and yet deeper, instead you will emerge at the gate. Whatever the Way, it has an interior, and it is sometimes a good thing to point out the gate. In strategy, we cannot say what is concealed and what is revealed. Accordingly I dislike passing on my Way through written pledges and regulations. Perceiving the ability of my pupils, I teach the direct Way, remove the bad influence of other schools, and gradually introduce them to the true Way of the warrior. The method of teaching my strategy is with a trustworthy spirit. You must train diligently. I have tried to record an outline of the strategy of other schools in the above nine sections. I could now continue by giving a specific account of these schools one by one, from the "gate" to the "interior", but I have intentionally not named the schools or their main points. The reason for this is that different branches of schools give different interpretations of the doctrines. In as much as men's opinions differ, so there must be differing ideas on the same matter. Thus no one man's conception is valid for any school. I have shown the general tendencies of other schools on nine points. If we look at them from an honest viewpoint, we see that people always tend to like long swords or short swords, and become concerned with strength in both large and small matters. You can see why I do not deal with the "gates" of other schools. In my Ichi school of the long sword there is neither gate nor interior. There is no inner meaning in sword attitudes. You must simply keep your spirit true to realize the virtue of strategy.

CHAPTER 5

THE BOOK OF THE VOID

The Ni To Ichi Way of Strategy is recorded in this the Book of the Void. What is called the spirit of the void is where there is nothing. It is not included in man's knowledge. Of course the void is nothingness. By knowing things that exist, you can know that which does not exist. That is the void. People in this world look at things mistakenly, and think that what they do not understand must be the void. This is not the true void. It is bewilderment. In the Way of Strategy, also, those who study as warriors think that whatever they cannot understand in their craft is the void. This is not the true void. To attain the Way of Strategy as a warrior you must study fully other martial arts and not deviate even a little from the Way of the warrior. With your spirit settled, accumulate practice day by day, and hour by hour. Polish the twofold spirit heart and mind, and sharpen the twofold gaze perception and sight. When your spirit is not in the least clouded, when the clouds of bewilderment clear away, there is the true void. Until you realize the true Way, whether in Buddhism or in common sense, you may think that things are correct and in order. However, if we look at things objectively, from the viewpoint of laws of the world, we see various doctrines departing from the true Way. Know well this spirit, and with forthrightness as the foundation and the true spirit as the Way. Enact strategy broadly, correctly and openly. Then you will come to think of things in a wide sense and, taking the void as the Way, you will see the Way as void. In the void is virtue, and no evil. Wisdom has existence, principle has existence, the Way has existence, spirit is nothingness.

Twelfth day of the fifth month, second year of Shoho (1645). Teruro Magonojo

THE FLOSS DUELLATORUM

Musashi's text on the subject of the art of the sword is not unique in its kind, but it does have previous examples in the West, particularly in Italy where, from the 10th-11th centuries, European princes or nobles were being trained thanks to the numerous schools that had sprung in every city or lordship. Towards the end of the 14th century, the figure of Fiore de' Liberi from Premariacco near Cividale emerged, he was a Friulian master-at-arms who composed an exceptionally thorough treatise on fencing in Italian and Latin, the 'Flos duellatorum' or 'Fior di battaglia', to this day the oldest and most extensive existing treatise . Fiore, whose personality and personal history were very similar to Musashi, had a predisposition for the martial arts from a very young age and began his training very young, also applying himself to the art of forging. Born in a multicultural land of the Holy Roman Empire, he had the opportunity to study and train with masters from both Italian and German areas, and in his travels he faced numerous challengers in duels, mostly motivated by envy and a desire for prominence. And frequently, in order to defend his honour, he was forced to fight against false fencing masters to whom he had refused to give lessons because they were deemed ninadequate or with inferior skills to any of his students. These duels were fought with long swords, without armour except for padded jackets and leather hand guards, and were all won without suffering any injury. Fiore de Liberi became famous in the courts of northern Italy for training famous condottieri and knights in duel, but his eclecticism also led him to take care of the maintenance of artillery pieces including crossbows and catapults that defended the city of Udine.

The Floss duellatorum was composed at the Este court in Ferrara around 1409-10 and has survived to the present day in only three manuscript copies, two in prose form kept in the Getty and Morgan private museums, and the third in poetic form in the Pisani-Dossi collection in Corbetta, Milan. The huge work is divided into sections that are not limited to the sword but range from bare-knuckle fighting to the use of the spear and is richly illustrated by painters of the time. In his manual, a veritable breviary on the craft of arms, Fiore provides instructions on fighting barehanded, on the use of dagger, one-handed sword and two-handed sword, gives advice on fighting with the sword while wearing armour, instructions on weapon axes, on the lance (on foot or on horseback), on the staff (a small stick similar to a club), and notions on fighting between duellists holding different weapons. This is how Fiore, in words typical of his time, presents the usefulness of the manual: "My friend , if you want to know how to practice with weapons learn all that this book teaches. Be bold in your assault and do not let not your soul seem old: Let no fear be in your mind; be on your guard, you can do it.

Let the woman be an example of this; fearful
And panic-stricken, she would never face naked iron.
So the fearful man is worth less than a woman;
Without audacity of mind everything would lack;
Audacity, that virtue, in particular, finds its place in art."
Each section explains the complexity of the instructions
with a group of Masters who at first demonstrate a type
of guard for the weapon they hold. They are then
followed by a master called "Remedial", who shows
how to defend against some basic attacks, and by
Scholari (students) who demonstrate variations of the
defensive techniques. Then a master called 'Contrario'
appears who demonstrates how to counter the moves
of the Remedial master or the Scholari. In some cases
another type of master, the Contra-Contrario, also
appears, explaining how to defend against Contrario.
The book's most famous illustration, the diagram of the
seven swords, presents the cardinal virtues of the
perfect fencer as the four indispensable gifts in the
European knightly world, depicting animals and objects
as metaphorical symbols, similar to Eastern traditions.
Prudence (a lynx holding a compass between its paws);
the ability to duel by reading the opponent's
movement, with continuous adjustments, to apply the
most correct defensive or offensive strategy.
Speed (a tiger with an arrow); combined with mental
and physical strength, to execute a combat technique
with lightning speed and to instantly interpret one's
opponent's   moves.
Audacity (a lion holding a heart under its right foreleg);

in constant struggle with the lynx because in order to win, courage and restraint must go hand in hand in an experienced and balanced fighter. Strength (an elephant with a tower on its back); basic stability combined with the use of the levers of the human body that have been forged to dexterity and technique.

Around the figure of a man, the seven swords represent the six cutting blows that can be done, either mandritti (blows that start on the side of the dominant hand and go in the opposite direction) or manrovesci (blows that start on the side of the non-dominant hand and go in the opposite direction); or two slashes (cutting blows that go from the top to the bottom), two mezzani (horizontal cutting blows), two sottani (cutting blows that go from the bottom to the top), and a point, placed centrally at the bottom. The culture of the sword in the West, in its concreteness, has always been more attentive to the external act, exalting the symbolism of the sword itself especially for religious purposes, while the Eastern culture gave great importance to the mental and spiritual state of the duellist intimately united with physical gestures. Western fencing and Japanese swordsmanship differed above all in their practice: in the former, one hand was used to defend oneself in order to be able to attack at the same time, while in Japan the sword was used with two hands, primarily to strike the opponent while exposing one's own body to his blows.

A Growth Path for the Man of Today This text, like Sun Tzu's "The Art of War", is the uninterrupted subject of study in all military academies as a fine treatise on strategy, whose intelligence, flexibility and firmness to be applied in a duel or on the battlefield are very appreciated.

Its success is not simply based on a forma mentis that combines psychological motivation and concentration to overcome the competitions of existence, of the "mors tua vita mea", because only at this level the bibliography in terms of literature and techniques of every time is very rich .

Therefore, starting from the evident cultural and almost anthropological diversity between Europeans and Japanese also in the spirit and art of the sword, what use can we take from this book for our "contingent"? And what is hidden behind the perfect skill acquired by dint of countless martial tests? There is always something tragic and inescapable in the Japanese narrative, which, coming from a sense of honour and loyalty, does not allow for hesitation. In this it is very close to the teaching of the Bhagavadgītā, the "Hindu gospel" where the god Krishna explains to Arjuna, hesitant to fight against the army led by his own relatives, how to get out of the ignorance that generates anguish, doing the duty assigned to him according to his own innate nature, without fear of sin. Musashi's soul is imbued with the concreteness of Zen Buddhism, but the Taoist influence is undoubtedly present, to which he refers in the chapter dedicated to the Void, claiming that the "profession of arms" is in fact only possible if one is on the Way, from which it is not possible   to   escape. Musashi knew well that one could not take the Void in itself and make it an object of knowledge, but knowing the existent, one can get to know the non-existent. Only by practising the way of the warrior, the way of Heiho, every day and every hour, without any backdown or sign of laziness, will it be possible to understand that "the mind is emptiness", that is, that a free mind in tune with the universe is capable of no longer dwelling, or rather of not attaching itself, to any one thing, but rather of penetrating everything indiscriminately: a vision that students should never forget.

Our path of reflection will therefore try to reinterpret the meaning of the five rings with as many vital elements hidden under Musashi's original words, willing to give them a new value, chapter by chapter, starting from more tangible aspects, gradually ascending (or descending if you prefer) towards our true being.

Among the disciplines which a samurai applied to in addition to the sword, he paid much attention to calligraphy (shodo), an art form three thousand years old. Sword and brush in the same way represented the artistic expressive tools of the warrior combining strength, delicacy, clarity, balance and sharpness. Musashi, in his mountain cave, intent as he was to giving sense and preciousness even to the beating of a butterfly's wings, was actually writing for the whole humanity and not only for those who approached the noble art of the sword; he was doing it so that the universal could be drawn from the particular, in war as in peace. His style was marked by balance, by the essential without frills, apparently simple but deep at the same time, typical of Haiku, the classic short poetic composition, intimately Japanese.

In being attentive to everything, vigilant in war as well as in peace, Musashi excluded discouragement or resignation; an approach of strength and daring intrinsic to countless characters throughout history, especially of a warlike nature. A concept that could be expressed with the same firmness even in a completely different context: Emily Dickinson, the great American poetess of the last century, who spent most of her life locked in her room, reminds us of it when she wrote in a fragment: "We never know our height until we are called to rise. And if we are faithful to our task comes to heaven our stature." Emily urged us to fight with our inner adversary, that lump of thoughts in which lack of purpose, materialism, individualism are tangled; the disturbing guest as the philosopher Umberto Galimberti renamed it in one of his books.

And it is our task only , as Kahlil Gibran warns us: "No one can teach you anything except what already lies dormant in the dawning of your knowledge. And just as each one is alone in the knowledge of God, so must he in solitude know God and understand the earth."

Musashi also invited to simplify, like the ancients, who wisely remembered that the simple is the seal of truth. Goethe noted that human beings cannot stand the simplicity of truth, it annoys them being instinctively led to an intellectual baroque that questions the many why we are here. Working to become simple is not easy and Jesus himself claimed that "if you do not become like children you will not enter the kingdom of heaven; so, cleaning our attention, not needing the "more", focused on every aspect of life we will not waste a single moment of it.

But probably the most profound teaching that Musashi suggests to us, starting from the bottom, firmly planted on the earth, in order to move spiritually towards the divine, is that "we must be both in the world and of the world", far from the thought of St. Paul, the true founder of Christianity. And we will try to follow this precious indication.

THE FIRST RING - THE RHYTHM

For Musashi in the empty mind of the samurai there is the rhythm of action, in success as in failure, in reaching the goal as in missing it, exercising the art of war with its infinite variations. Rhythm, from the Greek "rhythmos", which means measured movement, flow" implies a psychophysical harmony marked in the face of adversity, made of beauty, right time, speed, quiet, change.

We cannot disregard rhythm, we can change it, but not eliminate it; it is an integral part of our lives and actions, like breathing, indispensable to such an extent that Goethe said that "Rhythm has something magical about it; it even makes us believe that the sublime belongs to us."

A wonderful interpretation of rhythm is dance, which since the mists of time has been vividly present in the life of man, who has assigned it different meanings from time to time.

Shams i Tabrizi, Persian poet and philosopher of the thirteenth century, teacher of the great Jalal Al din Rumi, claimed: "Well-thinking and moralistic, narrow-minded people believe that dancing is a sacrilege. They think that God gave us the gift of music, not only the music we play with voices and instruments, but the music that underlies all forms of life, and then forbid us to listen to it. Don't they realize that all of nature sings? In the universe everything moves according to a rhythm: the beating of the heart, the wings of a bird, the wind on a stormy night, the blacksmith working the iron, the sounds that surround the unborn child in the womb... Everything participates, in a passionate and spontaneous way, to a unique and wonderful melody".

And this All in the rhythm probably reaches its peak in the dance of the rotating dervishes typical of Sufism. The Sufis, the Islamic mystical current, say that as a drop of sea water carries inside itself the whole ocean, so our dance reflects and hides at the same time the secrets of the cosmos, because the human being is nothing but an instrument in which God blows his own music.

It was Rumi himself, the greatest mystic of Islamic culture, who founded the brotherhood that represents the perfect way of conjunction between man and God in a whirling ritual of ecstatic trance called "samā". Fascinating is how it all began, in Konya in Turkey around the middle of 1200, in the testimony of one of Rumi's companions:

"A few hours before the performance, Rumi and I retired to meditate, and we were joined by the six dervishes who would perform that evening. Together we performed ablutions and prayed. Then we put on our costumes. We had earlier discussed extensively what was appropriate attire, and had chosen simple costumes in earth colours. The honey-coloured headdress symbolized the tombstone, the long white robe was the shroud, the black cloak, the tomb. Our dance represented the way Sufis get rid of the self, dropping it like an old dead skin....Turning himself over into the hands of God, the first dervish began to twirl, and the hems of his skirts came swirling to life as if they lived on their own. We all joined in the dance, spinning until all that remained around us was the presence of God. Whatever we received from the heavens, we passed on to the earth, from God to man. Each of us became a link that connects the Lover with the Beloved. As the music ceased, we all together bowed to the elements of the universe: earth, water, wind and fire, and the fifth element: emptiness."

We cannot fail to emphasize the perfect coincidence of the universal elements in the visions of Rumi and Musashi, as if they were one common feeling.

The theme of rhythm in the dance of dervishes was studied and taken up by the Armenian philosopher and writer Georges Gurdjeff who lived between the end of the nineteenth and the beginning of the twentieth century. He claimed that in learning the practice of dances, one gains access to a wider reality, alive and delightful, that makes one find its own center going inside oneself until one finds not a person but only pure presence, a living silence, sacred, full of its music, of its dance. And about dance he wrote: "You forget, you have no memory, you forget. You have to repeat, repeat, repeat. You have no power of concentration. It's the same for everyone. This is the purpose of the work. If a man could concentrate and keep his attention for only fifteen minutes or an hour without being distracted, he would be as great as your Notre Dame, as Christ. I would ask him to be my teacher."

THE SECOND RING - THE RITUAL

In the practice of Musashi's sword art it transpires that the ritual is perfection that strengthens us as the scrupulous and apparently mechanical repetition gives confidence to belong to the world: he seemed to embody the universe in action when fighting a duel. Already in the Rgveda, the most ancient text of Indo-European culture written in Sanskrit, the word "ritu" meant the immanent order of the cosmos, which is the universal law of Hindu dharma.

From this cosmic sense the religious meaning of the rite, common to all latitudes, originated, according to which, since the beginning, the celebration of one's own rites gave identity, unity, strength, sense of belonging and survival; a cohesion culminating in the "catharsis" in which (one's own) Truth is shared.

In every religion or belief, the ritual with its symbolic actions contains a powerful sense of the sacred and transcendent precisely because it is detached from daily life, it is an almost suspended moment, separate from it, awaited and lived with love. Many have wondered about its deep meaning at unconscious level , and while according to Freud the ritual exorcised fear, for Jung it had three meanings: to transform vital energy into spiritual energy, to establish its meaning, to have a saving effect on the soul under the religious aspect. In the essay "The symbolism of the mass" without doctrinal intentions, he stated that the mass "can be called a rite of the process of individuation, an experience that transmits the unity of multiplicity, the unique man in all" as a distinctive feature of the unconscious. Jung, as a former Catholic who became a Protestant, openly acknowledged the greatness of Christianity and especially Catholicism, greatness which other faiths do not have.

Being tribal, warrior, religious, of initiation, of passage, of seal to some brotherhood or order, the ritual is individual and collective, a necessary act of inner order that guides, orients and contains. It is a transformative experience, because as one leaves the sphere of the Ego to enter into contact with the Self in a reconstruction of meaning and sacredness in life. There is much of Musashi's thought in these words of Jung.

If ritual also favors the sense of community, Aristotele would have certainly rejoiced, as he claimed that "to live in the polis alone, either you are an animal or you are a god," because man is a political and social being who also feeds on rituals. Confucius was an ardent supporter of this as he was a skilled politician, considering the ritual an essential element to internalize and share ethical and moral values of rectitude and to harmoniously order the society.

The space of the sacred (from sacer, separate) was also defined through the ritual , as Romulus did in the legendary founding of Rome, when he delimited the limen,with plow and oxen, tracing a precise square which became a place of vital space from a first indistinct place , it became a templum where you could practice virtue.

The ritual is also "symbol in action", it is the metaphor of life that is activated with rhythm and established rules, with repeated acts and languages. Faced with the feeling of impotence, division, emptiness, which frighten existence, the ritual transforms the Kaos into Kosmos, making joy and inner peace flourish again. Beyond religious practices, Musashi insisted on the need to transform anything or any daily activity into a ritual with an almost sacred aura, as Mircea Eliade argued , the great historian of religions, who analyzing the ancients in their rituals observed: "by transforming all physiological acts into ceremonies, they tried to go beyond, to project themselves beyond time, into eternity".

Certainly, the ritual can fall into habit, becoming a purely formal and dutiful practice, devoid of the "numinous" character that celebrates life in every moment.

Benedict of Norcia reflected carefully on this , in his "Rule" he marked minutely and ritually the individual moments of the day of his monks under the famous motto "hora et labora". For Benedict, son of a time of great uncertainty and deep connoisseur of the human soul, rites were precious not only in order to live joyfully in a spontaneous and always new way the daily life, but to "prune" fears, depressions, jealousies, and defeat acedia, the greatest enemy of a monk, called the demon of noon, one of the seven deadly vices for Catholicism.

If after more than 1500 years the Rule preserves its vitality it is also because the rite takes place within a unique and circumscribed community, organized as a warrior body. It is not by chance that the Saint, in the chapter dedicated to the various types of orders, had no doubts: "the first is that of the cenobites, who live in a monastery, militating under a rule and an abbot".

THE THIRD LINK - SPIRITUALITY

Musashi always obeyed to a strict inner discipline according to which every little action or non-action, performed because it is right to do so, has a sacred aura, and its perfect execution affects the ethics of the self and of the world. The sacredness of the great Japanese master's thought can be found in Meister Ekkart, Dominican theologian and medieval mystic, who affected the German spirit as much as Dante, his contemporary, affected the Italian spirit. Recognizing mysticism as the highest form of spirituality, he was an authentic warrior of thought centered "on the soul that desires to be united with God, in equality with Him". In order to allow God to enter, the "creature", that is the ego, must come out, it must be annihilated: by practicing detachment, by becoming Nothing, by having nothing to defend, there will be the death of the flesh and the birth of the spirit. In this way it will be possible to love and forgive unconditionally, without any reason, like God who is Love.

Ekkart in his treatise "On the noble man" combines the "know thyself "at the base of the classical philosophy to the" know God", coming to claim that "the soul and God are one thing " because the logos is only one, human and divine. He was in fact accused of heresy (which in Greek means choice) and he believed that to every Christian should apply what Jesus says about himself: to be one with the Father, thus completely reversing the biblical dualism, according to which there is a God up there in heaven and a man down here on earth. When the inner man, completely detached, has renounced to himself emptying himself, he comes to discover the essence at the bottom of the soul where it becomes spirit, as God is spirit, and so "to be empty of everything means to be full of God".

The German master proposed an original theological solution in the dispute over free will and eternal salvation, between those who denied the importance of actions for salvation, leaning towards predestination, and those who, on the contrary, considered actions absolutely fundamental.

He affirmed, like drawing a portrait of Musashi, that "it was necessary to focus on the intention, not on the realization of the action". The noble man always has a pure intention for any action he performs; thus it is not the actions that sanctify him, but it is he who sanctifies the actions through his own will and his own work, even when they do not come to an end due to force majeure.

"One should not so much think of what one should do, but of what one is: if one were good, and good was our way of being, our actions would shine brightly. If you are right, your actions are also right. Those who are not of a noble nature, whatever action they perform, it is worth nothing".

Jewish wisdom expresses with the word "kavvanah" the same intimate attention and intention aimed at purifying the heart and not change God's will.

Musashi and Ekkart thought that the divine spark present inside us, left free to express itself without mediations and intermediate veils, was a source of clarity and purity of heart, but already the Christian gnostic thinkers of the I and II century A.D., had gone beyond considering it as an instrument of salvation in contrast with the traditional dual vision, which in the end prevailed. Numerous sayings of Jesus in the apocryphal texts, especially in those of Thomas, testified the divine inside us, and also for this reason were excluded from the definitive canon of the four gospels. And among them: "The kingdom of God is within you and outside you, it is all around you...not in temples of wood and stone. Lift a stone and I will be there, break a wood and you will find me"; and again, extolling its saving nature, "If you express it from yourselves, what you have will save you. If in yourselves you do not have it, what in yourselves you do not have will kill you."

Or by exhorting us to discover its wonder: "Let him who seeks not desist from seeking until he has found; when he has found, he will be amazed. When amazed, he will be upset and will dominate everything".

The samurai Musashi was in some ways a noble man in the highest meaning of Ekkart, a man who does not estrange himself from the world but sanctifies it through his own will, acting actively in it, helping it (as an example of virtue) without any egoic form, not running away from pain and suffering but rather taking charge of it.

Just as the Buddhist Bodhisattvas, or the ancient Rishis, the wise authors of the Hindu Vedas, acted in an even more loving way.

THE FOURTH RING - AWARENESS

Even spirituality is a momentary state of mind subject to interruptions and changes, which leads to flashes of happiness, even substantial but not permanent. Musashi, in his manual, clearly expressed that through awareness, that is the pure and total presence of being, one can fully express one's action, whether of martial nature or not. In the art of the sword as in the myriad of activities and daily thoughts it was a matter of performing a real overturning of their beliefs or certainties coming to understand that mind and body are part of the self and not the opposite. In order to reach this illumination, according to the Buddhists, one can follow two paths, the direct and the indirect. The latter consists in a gradual approach through beneficial meditation techniques such as yoga, reiki, qi gong and many others in order to pacify the mind: a way certainly useful for inner clarity but not definitive because the mind once "untied" from these conditioning returns to its tumultuous state. The direct way is based on recognizing "here and now" that there is no difference between subject and object as there is only "the experience in that precise moment", a way masterfully embodied by Musashi in facing his opponents in a duel. Awareness or pure consciousness is the only reality, like a screen is the only witness that attends the passage of events and the contortions of the mind with its thoughts, emotions, feelings and drives that constitute the ego. The ego mainly wants two things: on the one hand it continuously seeks limph to feed itself, feeding itself with ever new desires and expectations, on the other hand it resists and tends to escape, not wanting to inevitably die in front of the fundamental questions of the human being. In doing so, it acts as a separate self that shares nothing with the eternally present Self, indifferent to external stresses.

The great Taoist master Chuang-Tzu affirmed that "a great man is a man without ego",

suggesting the beauty of being once freed from this slavery. And in order to free himself from all conditioning, Manjushri, the Buddhist Bodishattva of wisdom, when asked about non-duality, went so far as to say: "do not speak of anything, do not give explanations, do not give indications, do not know anything, disregard all questions and answers".

Paradoxically, but not too much, we could find the most precious source in individuals who, although lacking in philosophical knowledge, have made an enormous impact with their teaching, such as the masters of Advaita Vedanta, an ancient current within Hinduism, centered on non-duality, which represents the culmination and the point of arrival in the path of knowledge of the Vedas.

According to Advaita, which in Sanskrit means "not two", man must tend to the fusion between our self (Ātman) and the great universal Self (Brahman): we are part of the whole and the whole is contained within us.

Sri Ramana Maharshi, a sage of the last century, spent a large part of his life at the foot of the sacred mountain Arunachala in India, and was a great interpreter of non-duality which he applied totally in his existence, long before he had read the ancient texts of Shankara which would have only confirmed his convictions.

All human beings wish to be always happy, far from pain, because this is in true human nature. It is a condition that we experience in the state of deep sleep, where the mind is absent, and which is reached through the Inner Quest, the direct way to free oneself and know oneself. The fundamental key to get in touch with our self is to ask "Who am I?" (Nan Yar in Tamil language), which is also the title of the only text personally written by Maharshi. He taught that in the swarm of thoughts the concept of "I" is the first one to appear in the mind and to which one clings, but when one constantly asks "Who am I?" all other thoughts dissolve and eventually the "I" vanishes, and what remains is the supreme non-dual Self. The false identification of the Self with the phenomena of the non-Self, such as the body and mind, at the end disappear and one reaches Enlightenment (Sakshatkara). Of course, while asking oneself "Who am I?", other thoughts pop into the mind and one should not make the mistake of getting caught but, on the contrary, one should ask oneself "To whom do they appear?". Maharshi therefore recommends to be extremely vigilant, always present, witness-observers, a pivotal concept in Musashi's thought that he always considered   a decisive conduct of life. Thus, the continuous questioning and investigation of oneself (anvē), will lead to a state of mental quietness, an exclusively functional mind, which is activated only when the situation requires it.

In an interview held with one of his students in 1902 to the question Who am I? The reply of Maharshi was:

"I am not the material body, which is composed of the seven humors; I am not the five sense organs, namely, the sense of hearing, taste, smell, touch and sight, which include their related objects, sound, taste, smell, touch and seeing; I am not the five cognitive organs, that is the organs of speaking, moving, touching, excreting, and procreating, which have as their respective functions speaking, moving, touching, secreting, and enjoying; I am not the five vital breaths which include the five respective functions of inhaling; I am not even the thinking mind; exactly as I am not memory, which pertains only to residual impressions of objects and in which there are neither objects nor functions." If I am none of these, who am I? "After denying all such things as "neither this", "nor that", (neti neti, in Sanskrit) only Consciousness remains - I am that." Which is the nature of Consciousness? "The nature of Consciousness is existence-consciousness-beatitude" (sat-cit-ananda).

What Maharshi said echoes perfectly in the words of Shunryu Suzuki, a Japanese master of the last century who brought Zen to the United States. In his famous text "Zen Mind, Beginner's Mind" he wrote: "In Zen we give importance to demeanor or behavior. By 'behavior' we do not mean a certain attitude that you must necessarily assume, but rather the natural expression of yourself. We give importance to spontaneity. You must be true in your feelings, clear in your mind, expressing yourself without reservation. This helps the listener to understand you more easily."

For Suzuki, practice and enlightenment are one and the same thing, and action emerges totally in the here and now, without a reason behind it but because of the fact of being in adherence with the situation. Not I, but this fact leads me to do, with spontaneity and simplicity, and so the same becomes favorable;

the same spirit with which Musashi intended and interpreted the practice of the art of the sword.

THE FIFTH RING - THE QUINTESSENCE

Musashi experienced in every moment rhythm, sacred rite, spirituality and awareness while dueling, meditating, simply living. In the silence of his cave broken only by the flowing of his brush on the paper, he felt the need to tend to the Void, almost subjugated in front of what cannot be described but only interpreted. For him, the Void to which he dedicated few but intense words in his fifth ring is "the Whole that contains everything", in the wake of many traditions both in the East and in the West: so for Taoism it is the Qi, for Christians it is the Holy Spirit, for the Jews the Ruah, for the Stoics the rational Logos or Pneuma, for Hinduism the Brahman, in the mathematical scientific vision it is the zero, a negligible nothing but in fact the basis of everything.

The great samurai in dividing his treatise on the art of the sword explicitly referred to the five elements that make up the world (Earth, Water, Fire, Wind and Vacuum), with a vision familiar to many schools of thought. In the Greek world, Aristotle added the ether as an astral element, eternal, immutable and incorruptible, to the other four material elements of the world such as fire, water, earth, air.

The same elements that according to the pre-Socratic philosopher Empedocles make all things exist, in arithmetic, geometry, medicine, psychology, alchemy, chemistry, astrology, divination and occult religion, in a concept of the universe based on the interconnection between its parts, (cosmogony). Even Ptolemy, the famous astronomer of the second century AD, made use of them by associating them with astrological signs.

In the Ayurvedic science everything in the universe is made up of five elements: ether, air, fire, water and earth; these are energies subtler than molecules and atoms themselves and together they give form to everything we see, animal and plants. According to Hinduism, all elements are created from akasha (the immense void, the ether) and everything reflects a part of God.

In the original Buddhism there are four elements that move all things: the earth represents solidity, water represents cohesion, air represents movement, fire represents temperature, while Tibetan Buddhism takes up Hinduism by adopting the five elements of which the Void is an integral part. In the Taoist conception, the interaction of the two opposites yin and yang through the elements, water, wood, fire, metal and earth, actually represents the five ways in which the movement of Qi is expressed, the vital energy that expands throughout the universe, in an eternal and harmonious cycle of existence that flows in the Way, in the eternal Tao.

The greek term aether became in medieval Latin "quinta essentia" (or fifth element), the deepest principle and ultimate foundation of all reality, the spiritus mundi of life and motion, divine nexus between individual microcosm and universal macrocosm.

The quintessence, in the Middle Ages and in the early Renaissance, as well as in astrology and naturalism, took on a deep alchemical meaning, well beyond its most common meaning of element capable of modifying metals to create the mythical philosopher's stone. An authentic alchemist was animated by a much higher purpose than the one of transforming matter and therefore also his own person in pure spiritual energy.

Having reached this point, we know that we are endowed with rhythm, we know the value of ritual, we are able to elevate ourselves to a spiritual state, aware of being aware. But (almost always) this is not enough for us, since we recognize the existence of a dimension of the spirit that overcomes us and that we are unable to understand; something that can make us permanently happy, like stabilitas, the cornerstone of the Benedictine Rule. We know that we are mortal, (the memento mori of our fathers), and we want to live in the best possible way this space of light that is granted to us. That's why we plunge into the self, meditating, doing yoga, listening to the breath, repairing the chipped aura, realigning the chakras, and doing much more with the intent of pacifying the mind.

At the same time, maybe not admitting it, we admire the granitic and dogmatic certainty of those who interpret faith in a strictly orthodox way (especially in the three monotheistic religions), a form that requires total commitment and devotion, trustingly surrendering themselves into the hands of a God who is radically something else; and this is really too much for us, we quickly become discouraged.

Charlotte Joko Beck founder of various Zen schools in the United States describes well the true condition of man in every age, especially these of today: "The things capable of upsetting the human being are millions, and they arise from a fracture when life ceases to be simply life, that is, seeing, hearing, touching, smelling, thinking; we dissociate ourselves from the undivided whole because we feel threatened, life goes where an unpleasant event occurred, and I think about it here to find a way out of suffering, and behind the search there is anguish and discomfort. Realizing that looking outside is useless and disappointing is a magical moment. The observer disappears because when nothing sees nothing, what is left but wonder? All that remains is life living, love and compassion."

One suffers because not being in the "here and now" uninterruptedly, the conscious presence is lost, the discriminating thought takes over and one returns to the subject/object dualism creating precisely the separation between the self and the reality which is the world or the flow of events. Objectively, it must be recognized that the "crisis of consciousness" catches us with great frequency and we discover that we are not in ourselves, or even "out of ourselves", so we must admit that the constant presence is the prerogative of few, of those who like Musashi have never been overwhelmed by an opponent, external and internal.

This is why we feel the deep need of a divine reality, of a cosmic design whose plot we do not know, but we are part of it, which we perceive in its transcendence but also in its immanence. A design that is the common denominator of the elements we have outlined in our journey, and that makes us accept reality as it is, recognizing that there is evil so that the good can exist , the unjust that makes the just subsist.

Knowing that everything happens because there is a meaning in the greater Meaning, strengthens us and conforts us when we feel there is no meaning in our lives. It is a moral duty to aspire to it according to Erich Fromm when he says: "Man's greatest task is to bring himself to light".

Musashi knew well that the virtues of a man, however noble, are not enough without understanding that they are part of a greater order that can guide, support and lead us in every circumstance towards happiness, the highest goal to which the human being tends; that path of harmony that the Japanese have always called ikigai.

In the three monotheistic religions the link between the self and the transcendent source is prayer, which represent for many believers the highest expression of inner healing and salvation. However, we are always in the presence of a dual form of approach to the world, where an ego is confronted with another self. Beyond extreme forms of asceticism where one experiences the ecstatic junction of one's soul with God, the concrete interaction of the individual who prays is to confront the divinity but not to incarnate it.

A different vision, not religious-dogmatic but spiritual and cosmic at the same time, is given to us by many spiritual traditions, especially Eastern ones, and by scientific and psychological research in the West. The eternal wisdom of the Tao shows us the way, flowing and floating in the events of life without resistance, as taught by Lao Tze in the Tao Te Ching, or as Chuang-Tzu reminds us in his Zhuang-Zi: "I follow the movement of water, not my will, that's why I can swim so well.

"Live with the gods happy in every moment for your fate as you accomplish whatever your dæmon desires," Emperor Marcus Aurelius echoes him, reminding us to be faithful to ourselves guided by the divine spark we have been given.

The Greek philosopher Plotinus, his contemporary, said "With our center we get in touch with the center of Everything", giving absolute preeminence to the One from which everything emanates and to which everything returns, for which nothing is governed by chance or material causes. The One as the summit of an ascending scheme that starts from the lower realities of the world, passes through metaphysics and the intellectual level, arriving at the supreme divine reality. Jesus himself, in the Gospel of Thomas, reminds us of the universality of the divine: "If your leaders tell you, 'Here is , the kingdom is in heaven,' then the birds of the air will be there before you; if they say to you, 'The kingdom is in the sea,' then the fish will be there before you. But the kingdom is within you and it is outside of you."

It is a vision enunciated as early as five thousand years ago in the sacred texts of the Vedas and then in the Upanishads, which finds in a thought of Shankara, Indian philosopher of the ninth century AD, the most admirable synthesis: "Only the absolute Brahman is real, this world is not real, the Ātman is not different from Brahman." According to the great master of advaita, ignorance (Maya) is at the root of non-knowledge (avydia), and like a veil prevents us from seeing universal reality for what it is, eternal and non-dual. This separation of the ego "makes us mistake a rope for a snake", and only the conjunction of identity between Ātman and Brahman (which is devoid of attributes) leads to the overcoming of the illusory reality of becoming in the eternal cycle of death and rebirth (samsara), achieving liberation (moksa).

The ancient Hindu vision had a powerful feedback and resonance in the Western scientific and psychological thought of the last century that questioned the unity of the universe.

According to Jung, synchronicity is the expression of creation, made of similar and attuned events and phenomena that attract each other in an unconscious relationship having the same end but not the same cause. They emerge from the personal unconscious which is part of a large collective unconscious, a common universal soul for which the world is nothing but an extension of us that puts together a multitude of events. In the process of individuation aimed at fully affirming the Self, or as Jung effectively said the "becoming self", the individual and collective dimensions share a mutual relationship in which one does not exclude the other.

An intelligent and universal law, which Plato already thought of when referring to the ideas that form material reality, which connected all the phenomena of nature by regulating the links between its parts. A soul of the world whose wonder Goethe exalted: "If the power of God did not live in us, how could the divine enrapture us"?

It is in quantum physics that fundamental steps forward were taken in the knowledge of the interconnection between entities. In a certain sense it considered "the universe as a giant living being", constituted by innumerable energies that aggregate in forms and frequencies interconnected in a precise and not random way; discovering how this works meant to unveil the secret of life.

Scholars and scientists including Plank, Sheldrake, Tesla, Hawking, Einstein, Schumann were focused on this theorem. According to Plank, matter does not exist as it is described, and everything is an interconnected vibration. Shaldrake described human beings as interrelated systems within further more complex systems in a universe of vibratory structures. Schumann mathematically discovered an electromagnetic frequency emitted by our planet, called the Schumann resonance, a constant vibration, like the breath or heartbeat of the Earth, so when we vibrate in unison we are "connected" and in relationship to it. Hawking was looking for a law of Everything, putting in relation the infinitely small of quantum mechanics with the infinitely large of Einstein's relativity.

Even the art gave its imprint and in particular with the genius of Raphael, when he painted The School of Athens he put at the center of the scene the two major interpreters of ancient thought surrounded by all the great philosophers of the time. Plato with his finger pointing upwards to indicate transcendence (the world of ideas, the Good) in a vision that went from form to content, while Aristotle with his arm in mid-air and his hand pointing down to emphasize the immanence of being, bringing content back to form. Raphael, son of the Renaissance that placed man at the center of the Universe, also intended to place at the center of everything the complementarity and coexistence of the two visions, as the quintessence of harmony and balance, It is the balance that gives light, Heidegger argued with the term he coined Lichtung (lightened, what is no longer hidden), referring to the metaphor of the clearing in the forest whose brightness is emphasized by the shade of the trees. This reciprocal bond that links everything to each other from the smallest particles, that makes us feel belonging to the Universe, gives purpose, elevates and highlights the preciousness of any human condition, contained in the Eternal Great Pre-existing Universal Soul. Rumi thought of this when he dictated the epitaph on his tomb: "When we are dead do not look for our graves under the earth, you will find them in the hearts of men."

Thanks.

We thank those who will have the goodness to read this text approaching in an unusual way to an exquisitely military text. If you feel like please leave a review that will be useful for us to improve our work. Thank you very much for your attention.

Bibliography:

Zhuāngzì - Chuang Tzu

The Tao - Jean Cristophe Demariaux

The Vedas - Giorgio Cerquetti and Parama Karuna Devi

Tao Te Ching - Lao Tzu

Of the noble man - Meister Ekkart

Being and Time - Martin Heidegger

Man and his symbols - Carl Gustav Jung

The naturalness of being - Jean Klein

Italy in 600 - Indro Montanelli and Roberto Gervaso

Life of St. Benedict and the Rule - Gregory the Great

Daily life according to Saint Benedict Lèo Moulin

Bushido the soul of Japan - Inazô Nitobe

The Gnostic Gospels - Elaine Pagels

The essence of the Bhagavadgita - edited by Paramhansa Yogananda

Enneads - Plotinus

The sandals of Abraham - Maria Rosa Poggio

The book of inner depths - Jalal al Din Rumi

Conscious Presence - Rupert Spira

THE BOOK OF FIVE RINGS

Who am I? - Sri Ramana Maharshi

Letters from vacuity - Shunryu Suzuki

The Art of War - Sun Tzu

Hagakure - Yamamoto Tsunetomo

The world system of modern economics - Immanuel Wallerstein

Printed in Great Britain
by Amazon